The Outsiders

Issues in Organization and Management Series
Arthur P. Brief and Benjamin Schneider, *Editors*

Employee Ownership in America: The Equity Solution
Corey Rosen, Katherine J. Klein, and Karen M. Young

Generalizing from Laboratory to Field Settings
Research Findings from Industrial-Organizational Psychology,
Organizational Behavior, and Human Resource Management
Edwin A. Locke, editor

Working Together to Get Things Done
Managing for Organizational Productivity
Dean Tjosvold

Self-Esteem at Work
Research, Theory, and Practice
Joel Brockner

Implementing Routine and Radical Innovations
A Comparative Study
Walter Nord and Sharon Tucker

The Outsiders
Jews and Corporate America
Abraham Korman

Organizational Citizenship Behavior
The Good Soldier Syndrome
Dennis W. Organ

Facilitating Work Effectiveness
F. David Schoorman and Benjamin Schneider, editors

Futures of Organizations
Innovating to Adapt Strategy and Human Resources
to Rapid Technological Change
Jerald Hage, editor

The Lessons of Experience
How Successful Executives Develop on the Job
Morgan W. McCall, Jr., Michael A. Lombardo, and Ann M. Morrison

The Outsiders

Jews and Corporate America

Abraham K. Korman
Baruch College

Lexington Books

D.C. Heath and Company/Lexington, Massachusetts/Toronto

The author and publisher express their thanks to those who have granted permission to reproduce copyrighted text. The copyright acknowledgments appear on page 197.

Library of Congress Cataloging-in-Publication Data

Korman, Abraham K., 1933–
  The outsiders.

  Includes index.
  1. Jews—United States—Economic conditions.
  2. Jews—Employment—United States.   3. Corporations—
United States.   4. Personnel management—United States.
  5. Discrimination in employment—United States.
  6. United States—Ethnic relations.   I. Title.
  E184.J5K777   1988   331.6′ 3′ 924073   84–40740
  ISBN 0–669–09987–2 (alk. paper)

Published simultaneously in Canada
Printed in the United States of America
International Standard Book Number: 0–669–09987–2
Library of Congress Catalog Card Number 84–40740

The paper used in this publication meets the minimum requirements of American National Standard for Information Sciences—Permanence of Paper for Printed Library Materials, ANSI Z39.48–1984. ∞™

89 90 91 92 8 7 6 5 4 3 2

Contents

Tables   ix

Foreword   xi

Acknowledgments   xiii

Introduction   xv

1. Jews as Outsiders in American Life   1

   The Importance of Being an Outsider: The Insider-Outsider
   Factor in Intergroup Relations   1

   Historical Sources of Jews' Outsider Status   4

   Jews in American Society   7

2. Jewish Americans and Entrepreneurial Occupations:
   A Success Story   17

   Why Entrepreneurial Careers? The Influence
   of Environmental Opportunity, Childhood Socialization,
   and the Outsider Factor   18

   Some Illustrations of Jews' Success
   in Entrepreneurial Careers   20

3. Managerial/Executive Roles: The Implications
   of Outsider Status   27

   The Significance of Social Acceptability in the Managerial/
   Executive Role   28

   The Impact of the Outsider Factor on Jewish Managers:
   Findings from Empirical Research   29

*Recent Investigations of Jews as Outsiders
in Corporate America 33*

*Further Evidence for the Outsider Hypothesis: An Interview
Study of the Role of Jews in Corporate America 35*

4. Jews and Corporate America: From Post–World War I
   to the Mid-1970s 43

   *Patterns of Jewish Employment in Corporate America:
   1918–41 43*

   *Patterns of Jewish Employment in Corporate America:
   From World War II to the Mid-1970s 47*

5. Jews and the Corporate Hierarchy:
   A Contemporary View 57

   Jewish Presence in the Corporate Elite 58

   *Proportions of Jewish Senior Executives: Overall
   Comparisons across Industries and Companies 61*

   *Jewish Presence in the Corporate Hierarchy:
   Industry Variations 65*

   *Industry and Company Variations in Jewish Presence
   at Senior Management Levels 66*

   *How Do Jews Become Chief Executive Officers
   and Members of the Board? Further Evidence
   for the Importance of the Insider-Outsider Factor
   in Executive Selection 84*

   Conclusions 87

6. Contemporary Corporate Patterns of Recruitment
   and Selection 91

   The Slavin and Pradt Studies of Corporate Recruiting 91

   Recruiting in the 1980s: A Follow-Up Analysis 99

7. Jews, the Professions, and Corporate America: Another
   Success Story 107

   *The Partially Closed Gates prior to World War II: Elite
   Colleges, Professional Schools, and the Quota System 108*

After the Gates Opened: Post–World War II 111

The Jewish Professional and Corporate America 114

*A Study of Industrial and Organizational
Psychology Professionals* 116

*The Impact of Professional Success: Expected
and Unexpected Effects* 119

*A Developing Problem: Declining Opportunities
in the Professions* 120

8. Economic Motivation and Insider-Outsider Status 125

*The Arab Boycott of Israel and Its Implications
for Employment of American Jews* 126

*When Financial Criteria Dictate Selection: Some Changes
in Commercial Banking* 130

9. Organizational Characteristics and Hostility
toward Outsiders 133

*The Effect of Hierarchical Status and Authority on Hostility
toward Others* 134

*Hierarchical Organizations and Intolerance of Outsiders,
Variations, and Differences* 136

10. Reactions to Equal Opportunity Programs:
The Internalization of Outsider Status 141

*Supreme Court Decisions, Equal Opportunity
and Affirmative Action Programs,
and Jewish Employment* 144

*A Case Study of the Effects of Affirmative Action Programs:
The Oil Industry* 147

*The Demonstrated and Potential Impact of Affirmative
Action Programs on Jewish Employment* 149

*The Paradoxical Reactions of Jewish Agencies
and Community Leaders* 152

The Acceptance of Outsider Status and Its Implications 154

An Integration 162

11. Some Thoughts about Change and Some
    Continuing Questions 165

  What Corporate America Can Do 166

  What the American Jewish Community Can Do 169

  Contemporary Anti-Semitism in the United States 173

  Resolving the Dilemma 180

  *Some Continuing Considerations
  for the Jewish Community 184*

  Conclusions 187

References 189

Copyright Acknowledgments 197

Subject Index 199

Name Index 201

About the Author 204

Tables

3–1. Summary of Findings: Perceived Impact of Being Jewish on an Executive Career, Compared to Other Religious Groups

3–2. Reasons for the Hindering Influence of Being Jewish on Executive Promotability

5–1. Relationship between Religious Affiliations of Philanthropists and Corporate Board Memberships

5–2. Industries with Low Proportions of Jewish Senior Executives

5–3. Industries with Percentages of Jewish Senior Executives at the Nationwide Norm

5–4. Industries with Above-Norm Percentages of Jewish Senior Executives

5–5. Within-Industry Company Differences in Numbers of Jewish Senior Executives

5–6. Percentages of Jewish Senior Executives in Fortune 100 Companies

5–7. Percentages of Jewish Senior Executives in Service-Related Industries

5–8. Percentages of Jews in Commercial Banking Top Management, According to Geographic Area

6–1. Recruiting Visits in the New York Area, 1972–73

6–2. Recruiting Patterns in the Mid-1980s

7–1. Employment Patterns for Jewish and Non-Jewish Industrial and Organizational Psychologists

10–1. Effects of Affirmative Action Programs on Levels of Minority Group Employment in Oil Industry Firms

10–2. Household Incomes as Percentages of Total, New York Metropolitan Area Jewish Population, 1981

11–1. Non-Jews' Beliefs about Jews in the United States

11–2. Beliefs about Jews in the United States: Black/White Comparisons

Foreword

Arthur P. Brief
Benjamin Schneider

No matter what group is the target, unfair employment discrimination is a repugnant phenomenon in America. Perhaps because race and sex are such visible signs of group membership, discrimination against blacks and women has received considerable attention in both the scientific and practitioner communities. Discrimination on the basis of religion, however, is a relatively under-attended-to social problem. Our hope is that Abraham Korman's book will help correct this relative imbalance through its focus on Jews in corporate America.

Korman's *The Outsiders* opens by recognizing the seemingly remarkable successes of Jews in what, at first, appears to be virtually every walk of American life. However, his subsequent historical analysis goes on to document carefully the absence of Jewish executives in major segments of corporate America. Korman does more than pinpoint where Jews have succeeded and failed. He also offers a rich social psychological explanation as to why, appropriately tempered by treatment of contemporary economic and political forces. Finally, Korman suggests ways in which the unfair employment discrimination experienced by American Jews may be alleviated. In doing so, he provocatively prescribes how organizations should change their employment practices, how public policies should be altered, and how the American Jewish community should adjust its reactions to anti-Semitic incidents.

While *The Outsiders* is a book about Jews, it speaks to all who care about justice in the workplace. By coming to understand better discrimination against Jews, one gains a greater sensitivity to the problems confronted by the many out-group members that help comprise America's labor force. It is for this reason we are particularly proud to have Korman's book as part of our series.

Acknowledgments

The completion of a book brings both intellectual and emotional reactions. There is the knowledge of completion of an effort that has been a dominant part of one's life for several years, a knowledge that brings both the joy of completion and the sadness of loss. "It is done" and "it is no more" are words but they signify reactions of a very complex nature and now that they are appropriate, the author can only hope that readers will find the material as important and as fascinating as he did.

There are many individuals who have contributed to this book and whom I would like to thank in this public forum. Art Brief and Ben Schneider, the academic co-editors of this series for Lexington Books, were the original sparks for the book and provided valuable critiques of the what-seemed-to-be innumerable drafts. Similarly, Bruce Katz and Bob Bovenschulte have represented the needs of Lexington Books in a meaningful manner and have done credit to the book publishing industry with their assistance, valuable critiques, and constant support throughout.

Also of importance in helping the book through its revisions were Dr. Yehuda Amir of Bar-Ilan University, Dr. Allen Weingarten of General Electric and Ms. Hadassah Linfield of the American Jewish Committee of Philadelphia, all of whom provided psychological support for the project as a whole and valuable critiques of the manuscript revisions. Throughout, there has been the assistance from my wife Rhoda and my children Scott and Stacey. All continually listened to my thoughts throughout the course of the writing and provided valuable feedback and information concerning matters about which I had some question.

Because of the contributions of these individuals and others too numerous to mention here, much has been added to this book that would have otherwise not been there. I hope they will be as satisfied with the results of their contributions as I am.

Introduction

Jews are among the most visible American minorities. They are among our most successful entrepreneurs, and they have built and managed many successful organizations. They have gained great prominence in such professions as medicine and law, and they are highly visible in the world of academia. They are among our most prominent writers, musicians, entertainers, and artists. As a group, Jews are above the national norm financially, and they are also increasingly prominent in the political spheres of American life at all levels—federal, state, and local.

Yet despite this visibility and economic success, and despite their overall contribution to the business community of the United States, the relationship between Jews as an American minority and corporate America has been and continues to be marked by complexities and paradoxes. One such paradox is that despite their prominence in entrepreneurial roles and in building and managing successful organizations, Jews have been and continue to be absent from managerial and executive roles in the overwhelming majority of the largest and most important organizations comprising corporate America. In industries ranging from oil to chemicals to foods to commercial banking and more—industries that have enormous economic and social power and that employ millions of people—there is a notable absence of Jews at senior management levels and, often, in management ranks in general. Yet, paradoxically, Jews are often found in these same industries in professional and staff positions, and they are frequently utilized as "outside professionals," providing various types of specialized assistance.

A further paradox in the relationship between Jews and corporate America stems from the societal and corporate programs of employment goal-setting and quotas for members of minority groups other than Jews and other American ethnic groups. Although some of these programs have been legalized by the Supreme Court, the impact of this approach to the employment process has gone far beyond the cases cited in such legal rulings. One effect of such differential recruiting, selection, and promotion practices has been to decrease employment opportunities for Jews and other Americans who work at various levels, including the professions, regardless of their demonstrated or predicted skills for the positions. A further paradox is that programs that have the effect of limiting professional and other job opportunities for Jews have been instituted, with rare exceptions, without significant reaction or protest from the Jewish community. Even more paradoxical is that these programs have often received significant support from agencies and prominent individuals identified with Jewish life in this country.

These inconsistencies between the successful history of Jews as entrepreneurs and their absence from managerial/executive roles in much of corporate America—as compared to their acceptance as professionals in the same setting and in the United States in general—are important because they tell us much about the American occupational opportunity structure, about where the structure may be working equitably and where it may not be. Also important is the paradox between the development and utilization of programs that limit employment opportunities for Jews and the lack of significant protest from Jews. Here, too, the inconsistencies are important because they relate to the issue of the fairness of career opportunity in the American work setting—which is the right of every American, Jewish and non-Jewish—and the conditions under which such equity may be attained.

These paradoxes are significant on several counts. Answers to them may help us understand the experiences of people who have contributed much to American society and corporate life in the recent past. Knowing what has happened to them as a result of the actions of others, and knowing how they may have contributed to these outcomes themselves, may help us understand how to help them and other groups who may be faced with similar problems in the years to come. The aforementioned inconsistencies are also significant for a corporate America that has found itself increasingly under severe competitive stress and that needs all the skilled talent potentially available to it at all levels, managerial and otherwise. Corporate America must answer, for itself and for others, why it apparently has not made optimum use of a potentially major source of talent. Finally, an understanding of these paradoxes will increasingly assume practical significance for coming generations of Jewish and other Americans as many of our traditional professions continue to decrease in market availability and potential value and as other potential careers assume increasing relevancy.

Organization of the Book

The overall goal of this book is to examine and provide evidence for these paradoxes, to outline their implications, and to suggest at least the beginnings of a change strategy. Chapter 1 begins by describing and defining the insider-outsider relationship in social behavior and the reasons for its usefulness as a framework for understanding intergroup relations. It will be shown that the more a person or group is seen as an insider, the more positive the affect and nature of the relationships involved. Conversely, the more a person or group is seen as an outsider, the more likely it is that the relationships will be negative. It is proposed that much of the occupational behavior of Jewish Americans stems from their status as outsiders in American life and that this status defines both the choices they make and the choices that others make about them. We will examine historical and contemporary evidence supporting this view of Jews as outsiders in American life and evaluate the degree to which such evidence supports historical perspectives and the continued popularity of such perceptions today.

The occupational and career implications of the perception of Jews as outsiders becomes our focus of concern in the following chapters. The discussion begins by showing how the success of Jews in entrepreneurial roles can be understood as a result of the juxtaposition of three important factors: the needs of American society for business growth and innovation, the traditional socialization patterns of Jewish Americans, and the outsider status of Jews in American life. All of these factors are seen as underlying the relative success of Jewish Americans in entrepreneurial roles. Paradoxically, however, we then show that it is this outsider status that has resulted in a reluctance among the overwhelming majority of corporate employers (except those controlled by Jewish families) to recruit, select, and promote Jews for careers—such as managerial and executive positions—that call for insider status and social acceptability. With a further paradox supporting the crucial significance of being viewed as an outsider, the analysis goes on to show that corporations have been far more willing to recruit Jews for roles that do not have great degrees of organizational power, such as staff and professional positions. Since these differential corporate hiring patterns are highly consistent with the attraction that Jews in this country have traditionally exhibited toward the professions—because of their self-directed nature and their requirements for skill and knowledge rather than social acceptability—a suggestion is made that there may have been (and may still be) a mutual pattern in which both corporate America and Jewish Americans have reinforced the same occupational choice patterns among upwardly mobile members of this group. In support of this argument, the discussion then reviews the great attractiveness of the professions to Jewish Americans and their considerable success in these roles compared to their relative absence in most of corporate America. Furthermore, it is also suggested that, possibly as a result of this interactive pattern, Jews in this country continue to see professional occupations as major career vehicles for upward mobility, even though there is some indication that the opportunities available in these careers may be declining.

We then examine the implications of the outsider status of Jewish Americans in corporate America in terms of its possible sanctioning of discriminatory actions against such individuals. One such instance is the interaction between economic opportunity and outsider status. Such interaction, it will be argued, may lead to an increased willingness to discriminate against Jews in order to attain economic benefits or, under other conditions, to an increased willingness to hire them. The basic rationale utilized here is that as outsiders, Jews do not receive the benefits of being "members of the family." Hence, affiliative considerations are irrelevant for them, and the major factor underlying interaction with Jews may be economic considerations. A second examined instance of possible discrimination as a result of outsider status is the increasing likelihood of serving as a target for discriminatory actions in organizations that are essentially hostile to those who are different from the norm in some way. In this discussion, it is proposed that the view of Jews as "different" in work organizations may have made them a more appropriate object of hostility (along with other outsiders) for those who work in hierarchical organizations that seem to encourage hostility to those who are different.

The discussion then turns to an examination of a most important paradox: the acceptance (and sometimes encouragement) by significant segments of the Jewish American community of programs that may have unfair discriminatory impact on their employment prospects. In attempting to explain such acts, it is proposed that the key here may be the tendency of Jews to view themselves as outsiders in American settings. Such self-views may underlie the apparently strategic decision among significant segments of the American Jewish community to combine forces with other outsider groups in American life in accepting and even encouraging programs designed to bring all "outsider" levels into line with one another, even if such programs may operate to the disadvantage of some members of the Jewish community.

The analysis concludes with a detailed examination of how the view of Jews as outsiders in corporate America has operated to the detriment of both parties and of American society in general. Finally, changes are proposed, according to two key themes: (1) the need to emphasize growth and personal responsibility on the part of any individuals to be helped by a change program, and (2) the need for us as a society, Jews and non-Jews, to be more willing to recognize and value the joys and benefits of being different and not to focus only on the problems.

1
Jews as Outsiders
in American Life

Two key factors underlie the relationship between Jews and American society—and, by extension, the American corporate community. One is the continuing belief shared by most Jews and non-Jews that despite their success as a group, Jews are still intrinsically outsiders in the American culture and in the American work setting and will continue to remain so, regardless of whatever occupational success they may attain. The foundation of this perspective is the historical anti-Semitism that we inherited as a nation from Europe and other cultures and that eventually also showed itself in American life—though in a considerably less virulent form. It is also a view that continues to be reinforced today by the sometimes different behavior patterns of Jewish and non-Jewish Americans in terms of religious observance and customs, holidays, dietary preferences (in some cases), and, often, political values.

A second key factor in understanding the relationship between Jews and corporate America is the behavior and attitudinal significance of outsider status. It is a status that has important implications for all parties involved—those who are the outsiders *and also those who are the so-called insiders.*

The Importance of Being an Outsider: The Insider-Outsider Factor in Intergroup Relations

All groups . . . develop a way of living with characteristic codes and beliefs, standards and "enemies" to suit their adaptive needs. The theory holds also that both gross and subtle pressures keep every individual member in line. The in-group's preference must be his preference, its enemies his enemies. (Allport, 1954, p. 38)

Inter-group conflict can be caused without differences in the material interests of groups. Tajfel proposed that the simple fact of belonging to a group was significant for group members in terms of social identity. Brought into interaction, or even just the presence of another group, members will tend to evaluate their own group in positive terms and the out-group in negative terms. Also, they prefer to interact with and reward their own group members. This, Tajfel suggests, is sufficient for conflict to occur, through discrimination and reduced interaction with the out-group. . . .

Identification with a group can be sufficient to cause discriminatory behavior between groups, and we can infer that the discrimination may exacerbate existing tensions. (Hartely, 1984, pp. 167–68)

Classifying people as insiders or outsiders appears to be a key factor underlying our liking, accepting, and feeling positive about some people but not others. We like insiders, or those whom we perceive to be like ourselves, more because we believe that they think the way we do. These beliefs make us feel less anxious around such people. People seen as insiders are more predictable and understandable, and because they are easier to anticipate, they are easier to work with. This positive feeling also builds other positive feelings. Since the relative lack of anxiety when we are surrounded by insiders makes us feel more positive about ourselves, we come to see ourselves as stronger, more virtuous, and more desirable, and as a group whose norms are worth following.

Outsiders are viewed as the opposite of insiders. Since they are less predictable, they make us feel more anxious and, therefore, less desirable and less virtuous. We accept them less and like them less because of the disquiet they raise in us. Furthermore, our perceptions of outsiders and insiders are likely to be become strengthened over time in the directions of our already formed opinions. The acts of the outsider tend to be perceived in a negative fashion, whereas the acts of a member of one's own group tend to be perceived positively.

The nature of such distortions may vary, however, depending

on the relative strength and power of the two groups. If the two groups are relatively equal in strength and power, they will grow further and further apart, eventually becoming polarized into two separate ways of thinking, behaving, and acting upon the world and each other. As they become more separated from one another, each becomes, in effect, a separate insider group that values its own way of thinking and acting while increasingly viewing the other group negatively. The process is different, however, if one group is stronger and more populous and has greater power than the other. Under these conditions, the larger group becomes more legitimate and more accepted as the "insider" group overall, and its norms, values, and perspectives are more sanctioned, officially and unofficially. Under these conditions, the smaller group becomes the "outsider" group and is increasingly treated as such. In brief, the smaller group eventually comes to adopt the view of the larger, dominant group, and its members come to see themselves as outsiders, just as they are seen by the insiders. Because of the power and strength of the insiders and because of the actual and/or potential use of sanctions this power implies, agreement develops between the two groups. Both see the larger, dominant group as insiders, both see the smaller group as outsiders, and the latter group is continually subject to the actual or potential power of the former. One result of such a pattern is that in order to increase its chances for survival and growth, there is a need for the outsider group to develop strategic responses to the potential and actual power of the stronger group. Sometimes the strategic response will be an identification with the insider group by adoption of their values and perspectives. Sometimes the strategic response will be an alignment with other outsider groups to be more effective in combating the demands of the stronger insider group. At other times, there may be withdrawal from the behavioral arena in which both groups operate, and the outsiders may eventually carve out a world of their own, where the insiders will not interfere with their activities.

Much of the patterns of relationships between Jews and corporate America may be viewed as reflecting the behavior of an outsider group in American society that is numerically smaller and less powerful than the dominant Christian society around them. As we will explore in considerable detail in the following chapters, Jews have been treated as an outsider group by much of corporate America, and Jews have reacted as an outsider group by adopting a number of the aforementioned strategies for responding to a numerically stronger insider group.

Historical Sources of Jews' Outsider Status

The view of Jews as outsiders in American life is pervasive in our history and continues to manifest itself today. It has appeared in our literature, in our business patterns, in our intellectual life, in our religious traditions, and in virtually all facets of our cultural life over the years, and it has remained intrinsic to American society. This view, which serves as the essential foundation of the view of Jews as outsiders in corporate America, stems from historical influences that continue to manifest themselves today and is continually reinforced by various aspects of our contemporary lifestyles.

The major source of the view of Jews as outsiders in American life is the two thousand years of European culture that has been our heritage and the anti-Semitism that was intrinsic to that culture. Although our country has been spared the violence that often marked European anti-Semitism over the years, it did inherit some aspects of these views, and the views continue to manifest themselves to the present day.

Here we can only provide the barest outline of this heritage and its manifestations, for it would be impossible in the space we have available to provide a full analysis of how deeply entrenched and historically supported this view of Jews as outsiders is in Western life. There are thousands of volumes on the origins, manifestations, and implications of the historical relationship between Jews and European culture, and thousands more will undoubtedly be written. However, brief as it is, we do need to provide such an outline if we are to develop an understanding of the historical place of Jews as outsiders in Western life and the reasons for the continued manifestations of such a view today, both in the American work setting and elsewhere.

For approximately seventeen hundred years, Christianity in its various forms was the overwhelmingly dominant religion of Europe. As a result of such preeminence, the leaders of the Christian faith were able to exert virtually total control over members of the Jewish faith—including, at times, the power of life and death. Frequently, such control took the form of hostile actions. Usually citing as justification for their actions the Jews' lack of recognition of Jesus as the Messiah—which was unacceptable to the Christian leaders—a common way to vent such hostility was to demand that Jews leave the country or locality. Historical data indicate that such expulsions took place in virtually every European nation in which Jews lived during the past two millenia. Jews were expelled from England in 1290 and from France twice during the fourteenth century (1306 and 1394). Similar expulsions took place in Hungary (1349 and 1360), Austria (1421), Lithuania (1445 and 1495), Spain (1492), Portugal (1497), Bohemia and Moravia (1744–45) and in various cities in Germany between 1300 and 1500. Also, Jews were not allowed into Russia for over two hundred years (until 1772), and when they were finally permitted to settle there, they were forced into one area, the Pale of Settlement. Even when Jews were allowed to remain in a country, the situation was frequently little better, since Church law often strongly regulated the degree and nature of the relationships between Christians and Jews. It is a tragic footnote to history that these same regulations were eventually taken over, virtually word for word, by the Nazis in preparing the world for their wholesale slaughter (Hilberg, 1961).

At other times, the hostility between the Church leaders and the Jews was less severe, and there were many years when the Jews of Europe lived in relative safety in such nations as the Netherlands and Italy. Almost always, however, regardless of when and where they lived, Jews, few in number, were constantly reminded of their outsider status and their lack of power relative to the dominant Christian cultures. Sometimes they were herded into ghettos, sometimes they were prevented from entering colleges and the most prestigious occupations, and sometimes they just had their possessions taken away arbitrarily. Regardless of how benign a particular situation might have been at a particular time—and benign situations did occur from time to time, despite the overall pattern of European history—there was always the knowledge that all could be lost in a moment—possessions, family, and, of course, life itself.

Further adding to such anxiety was the knowledge that feelings of outsider status and its negative implications were almost always justified, regardless of the type of Christianity being practiced in a country or, for that matter, the political values of the government. Although Martin Luther differed greatly from Roman Catholic views regarding Christian theology, he had similar views of the Jews as outsiders in European life. The writings of well-known Enlightenment and European political figures also showed that one did not have to be a religious Christian to have these views. Although they differed from Christian teachings in virtually all aspects and viewed the Church as an enemy, Enlightenment writers such as Voltaire, Fichte and d'Holbach also perceived the Jews as outsiders in European life who deserved all the enmity they received. The same was true of both the political left and the political right. Karl Marx's views of Jews were little different from those of the traditionally rightist conservative Christian churches and rightist political movements. The father figure of socialism believed that Judaism should disappear; he was so outspoken in his views that he was quoted by Hitler in later years. Also strongly concurring in this negative view of Jews as outsiders were such well-known socialists as Proudhon-and Engels. In the same vein, in recent years, the Soviet Union has relegated Jewish culture and Jewish theology to illegal outsider status; they are not to be taught or practiced.

It is significant that these European views of the Jews as outsiders remained strong over the years despite the adoption by different segments of the Jewish community of a variety of strategic responses in response to such status. While one segment followed what we may term the "Orthodox" response, which was to turn inward even further and thus solidify their "different" status even more, others went in the opposite direction. Typified by the growth of Reform Judaism in Germany and later in the United States, this strategy involved looking for ways to decrease differences from the surrounding community by adopting a wide variety of behavioral norms from the surrounding context. Yet the latter strategy fared little better in terms of the acceptability of Jews within the European setting. As events showed in the years prior to World War II and during that conflict, Judaism as a religion and the Jews of Europe as a group remained far more unitary in the views of others than might have been indicated by the very real religious and/or behavioral differences that had actually developed among them over the years as a group attempting to overcome the negative implications of their outsider status.

In recent years, there have been some remarkable positive changes in the status of Jews in Europe and in how they have been viewed by others. The systematic violence has pretty much disappeared, and there have been some significant changes in the attitudes and behaviors of the Christian churches of Western Europe toward Jews. The ancient libel of deicide has been eliminated; steps have been taken to either drop or change other aspects of Catholic theology that have been particularly troublesome for Jews; and there have been such dramatic steps as the Pope's visits to Auschwitz and to a Roman synagogue. There have also been positive changes in the laws of various European nations relative to the official position of Judaism, and most church officials, regardless of denomination, have been among the leaders in condemning the outbursts of European anti-Semitism that still occur. Despite these positive signs, however, strong outbursts continue to take place, and there is little indication that European nations, with the possible exception of some segments of West Germany, have fully come to grips with the implications of their own history relative to anti-Semitism and their documented complicity, at times, in Hitler's Holocaust. Indeed, a recent article by Miller (1986) has suggested that there is an increasing degree of amnesia regarding these events in some West German and French circles. In brief, the view of Jews as outsiders in European society continues to be pervasive and continues to cause them to be treated as outsiders. And the more people are treated as outsiders, the more they are perceived by others and by themselves as such.

Jews in American Society

Although Jews have been viewed as outsiders from the beginnings of the American nation, the eventual behavioral implications of the views that developed here became less virulent than those in Europe for at least two reasons. One factor has been a constitutional system that has separated church and state. Thus, the power of the religious doctrines that had such major impact in European societies was mitigated here by the lack of governmental support. Second, from the beginning, there were population differences between the European nations and this country, since those who came here were not a random sample of the nations they came from. Although it is likely that only a small number of non-Jewish migrants left Europe because of the anti-Semitism that pervaded that continent, it appears probable that they were generally less susceptible to European values and folkways than those who chose to remain.

As a result of these two major facts of American life, the history of Jews in this country has always been different from their history in Europe. One difference is that the view of Jews as outsiders in the major life of the country has not, with the exception of an isolated case in Georgia in the early twentieth century, resulted in the violence so common in Europe through the ages. Actions resulting from this view of Jews as outsiders in American life have been of another type, as illustrated by events that took place even before the American Revolution. For example, in the first recorded (attempted) official act of anti-Semitism in this country, the governor of New Amsterdam (the name of New York before it was taken over by the British in 1664) objected to taking in a boatload of Sephardic (Portuguese and Spanish) Jews escaping from the Inquisition. Also stemming from that era, but lasting as late as 1800, were the requirements of some states that office holders take Christian oaths of office. Perhaps most famous, however—and certainly much more important in its impact—was an incident that took place over a hundred years after our founding as a nation and that some consider as signaling to the growing nation the social acceptability of the view that Jews should be "kept out" of important areas of American life. Whether or not the incident deserves this notoriety, the exclusion in 1877 of Joseph Seligman, a wealthy New York Jewish businessman, by the Grand Union Hotel in Saratoga, New York, *was* an important event, and it apparently became a sort of signal to other hotels and various forms of social institutions. From that time on, keeping Jews on the outside, as well as more direct forms of anti-Semitism, became more and more common and had a major impact on the economic and social life of the country. One such area of impact was the immigration legislation of the 1920s and its explicit intent to minimize the number of Jewish and other immigrants from Southern and Eastern Europe and to maximize immigration from those nations where there were more potential immigrants of "traditional" American stock (for example, Northern and Western Europe). Also important during these years was the impact of Henry Ford's support of anti-Semitic publications. Ford was the most important business leader in a country that considered business its most important activity, and his support of anti-Semitic libels during those years was indicative of the view of Jews as somehow outside the mainstream of American life.

Further evidence for the pervasiveness of the idea that Jews were outsiders in American life and not worthy of the same consideration as those who could be considered "insiders" is found in the actions of the Roosevelt administration and the American media during World War II. Just as Japanese Americans were sent to internment camps on the basis of security considerations while Americans of German or Italian descent were not, the evidence is clear that the concerns of Jews were not considered relevant by the political and governmental leaders of American life or by the media. A number of studies in recent years have documented a lack of interest and lack of concern in the Holocaust among leaders of the American government, non-Jewish and Jewish, and among the American media, both immediately prior to that horrible event and while it was taking place. The record is now clear that both the Roosevelt government and the American media, written and visual, had knowledge of the Holocaust while it was taking place, but neither did much about it (see Lipstadt, 1985; Wyman, 1984). Also indicated in these accounts is the belief of some Jewish leaders that their status as outsiders in American society made them unable to call upon the Roosevelt administration for greater action.

The view of Jewish Americans as outsiders during this period was not limited to the government or media. Evidence abounds that this view was common, even among those from backgrounds supposedly dedicated to the reduction of bigotry and discrimination and to an increased understanding and acceptance of all peoples. The following quotations from well-known behavioral scientists of the time illustrate how deeply embedded was this view of Jews as outsiders in American life:

> "The practices of the Orthodox Jewish faith, by emphasizing the different culture of the Jew, enhances anti-Semitism," J.F. Brown, chief research psychologist of the Menninger Clinic, explained in 1942 in a paper "The Origin of the Anti-Semitic Attitude." "The costumes of the rabbis, the celebration of the chief feasts, especially the Sabbath, on other dates than those of the Christian culture, prohibitions regarding diet, the facade of synagogues—all mark the Jew out." The "only way" to counter anti-Semitism, Brown concluded, would be for Jews to surrender their religion, their customs, and anything else that marked them off from others and disappear into the crowd. "Responsible" Jewish leaders, he added, should not only urge "immediate cultural and final racial assimilation" but also do what they could "to discourage the entrance of Jews into those businesses and professions which are now 'over-populated' with Jews, and distribute them . . . into others which are 'underpopulated'." In another essay, . . . Talcott Parsons of Harvard, who was to become the most influential American sociologist of our time, explained that a major reason for anti-Semitism was the "over-sensitiveness to criticism" and "abnormal aggressiveness and assertiveness" that American Jews displayed. The "chosen people" idea is another source of friction. . . . Gentiles usually resent the arrogance of the claim that a group who are in a sense "guests" in their country claim a higher status than a "host" group. What is significant here is not Parsons' dislike of the concept of chosenness . . . but the way he defined the position of Jews in American society: they were guests in his country and would be well advised to behave like guests instead of acting as if they belonged here. (Silberman, 1985, pp. 56–57)

Two themes are apparent in these writings. The first is that Jews are "guests" in this country because they are "different." A second theme is that if they are being treated badly, it is their own fault for being different from the norm. Hence, if they want to be treated in a more satisfactory fashion, they have to stop "acting differently." Encapsulated in both these themes is the overall argument that Jews are outsiders in American life and that this is why they are viewed and treated negatively. In other words, according to these arguments, the victim is at fault for being different; the aggressor bears no responsibility, and it is up to the victim to stop being an outsider and change his or her characteristics if the negative views and the negative behaviors are to change. These are characteristic themes found in the literature of aggressor groups in defending the fact that so-called outsider groups are being treated badly as a result of such status. It would be hard to find stronger support for the logic and arguments underlying the significance of the insider-outsider factor in its impact on intergroup relations.

Coming up to the present day, perhaps the most appropriate way to describe the years since World War II and the situation in the 1980s is the French saying: The more things change, the more they stay the same. Clearly, Jewish Americans are highly prominent and successful as a group in the United States in ways they were not previously. They feel freer to protest, to voice opinions, and to articulate their emotions and their attitudes. The strongly voiced protests to President Reagan for his 1985 visit to the Bitburg cemetery, where Nazi soldiers were buried, would probably not have taken place forty years ago. In this way and others, the situation in the 1980s is different from the atmosphere during World War II. The Jewish American community is stronger, more powerful, and more willing to state their views.

However, money and success and prominence are not the same as social acceptance and the achievement of insider status. The fact that Jewish Americans have achieved such a level of prominence as a group is a sign of the increased openness of the American society, particularly since the World War II era. On the other hand, such growth in status as defined by economic criteria is not the same as social acceptance, and the two should not be confused. There is much evidence that even individuals who are successful in the attainment of economic criteria are often no more accepted socially; sometimes, the opposite is the case. At the very least, the assumption made by some that money operates like some kind of "magic"—such that the success of Jews as a group in an economic sense has led to greater social acceptance—is extremely difficult to support. In fact, there is considerable evidence that the view of Jewish Americans as outsiders in American life continues to be pervasive and intrinsic to much of our society.

One basis for this statement is the belief among many that America is a Christian nation and should remain so. In fact, this belief has apparently become even stronger in the 1980s with the growth of the "Christianization of America" movements. The degree of support for these movements, at least at this writing, is controversial. Some claim that they have been able to garner open support only among a small minority of Christian American religious and lay people. Others cite a figure of 20 million or more—about 20 percent of the American electorate (Morse, 1987). Regardless of the actual figures involved and the question of how one defines support, it is clear that changes have already taken place in American life as a result of the efforts of the Christianization movements. The Supreme Court has allowed the placement of a nativity scene on public land despite its religious significance; a court in Tennessee has allowed the censorship of books such as *The Diary of Anne Frank* on the grounds that they are offensive to the Christian faith; and there are now political candidates running for president and other offices on openly "Christian" platforms. Also, in 1984 the Republican Party thought of supplying all delegates to its National Convention with copies of the New Testament, a plan later discarded after protests by Jewish and other groups.

Less overt than the Christianization movements but also having implications in the same direction are those groups looking to break down the barriers between church and state. Among the demands of these groups are the introduction of prayer into the schools, tuition tax credits for private (including religious) schools, and the requirement that schools teach religiously based interpretations of human creation as well as the theory of evolution. Although these movements are not overt Christianization movements, they are viewed by many Jews as having similar impact, since any attempt to break down the barriers between church and state will inevitably, because of the discrepancy of the numbers involved, lead to a legalized legitimation of Christian religious perspectives as the "appropriate" values for American life.

Also symbolizing the continuing view in many circles of Jews as outsiders in American life are the contemporary manifestations of the medieval myths of Jews as some type of "secret, secretive, clannish, mysterious" group, with ways mysteriously different from that of "most Americans." As absurd as they may seem, these conspiracy views continue to be manifested in some of the respected areas of American life. Consider, for example, a recent article in *Business Week,* one of our most respected business publications. It is a magazine looked to by millions of readers for reports and interpretations of events in the world of business and in areas of governmental policy that have implications for the world of business. Yet in an article on illegal insider stock market trading in the September 8, 1986 issue, reference was made to the fact that some of the individuals linked to a major figure in such trading were Orthodox Jews who lived in Borough Park in Brooklyn (a major center of Orthodox Jewish life), that they might have been involved in other securities violations (although no evidence was cited) and that Orthodox Jews were a close-knit group who shunned relationships with outsiders and passed large sums of money around to one another and that such characteristics of Orthodox Jews had apparently hampered SEC investigators.

> In SEC testimony, Berel Light, who lived in Borough Park, described numerous loans, many in six figures, to and from friends, relatives and religious groups. Light said he did not know how his borrowers used the money. His attorney explained that "within the Orthodox community there is a certain feeling of helping each other, and they take care of each other financially and do not seek aid from other people."
>
> Some investigators say that such ties both facilitated the flow of deal information and compounded the SEC's difficulty in penetrating the network. (Source: Welles, Templeman and Cahan, 1986, p.77)

One wonders about the purpose of such comments as these. Why the use of such innuendos as "some," "many," and "are said to be"? What do they mean? Why the evoking of the imagery of some secretive, shadowy group outside the mainstream of American life? (Shades of medieval times!) Are the authors seriously proposing that the possible actions of a few individuals can be attributed to nearly a million Orthodox Jews? Are the authors seriously proposing that there is something in Orthodox Jewish tradition that leads to this type of behavior? Are they proposing that all Hasidic or Orthodox Jews are wealthy—a claim that would astound the many members of those groups whose income is far below our national median levels? Why the evoking of an imagery of a group outside of American life and, at the least, a less desirable group?

Also contributing to this continuing view of Jews as outsiders in American life is the "nativist" tradition in American literature, a perspective that is not limited to writers but is often articulated by them and that has influence far beyond their efforts. One recent manifestation of this view is an attack by the writer Gore Vidal on American Jews who support Israel. Calling them "fifth columnists," Vidal warned Jews that they were not "real Americans," as he was, and that they were only tolerated guests in this country. Vidal's attack on American Jews as outsiders reflects a characteristic that has pervaded the nativistic views of some of America's most famous literary figures since the founding of the nation. Irving Howe, a well-known writer himself, describes such views as follows:

> Vidal represents a kind of American nativism which goes back to Henry Adams and no doubt before. This is a feeling of resentment at the intrusion of immigrant communities or ethnic groups that violate the purity of American life. In expressing this nativism, Vidal picked on the Jewish issue, the Israel issue, the so-called dual loyalty issue. . . .
>
> He's asking for a monolithic outlook, a monolithic style. It's an anti-pluralist kind of thing.
>
> Behind this is an idea with a long history, going back, as I said, to Henry Adams. The idea is that the Jews somehow contaminate the language, the sensibility, the purity of national life. Besides, there has always been a sort of respectable anti-Semitism in this country in some segments of the upper Wasp community. It's not the real anti-Semitism of people who want to kill you. It's the anti-Semitism of people who just don't want you to come around to their club. (Grossman, 1986, pp. 17–18)

Also contributing to this view of Jews as outsiders in contemporary America is that there are often real differences in customs and values between some Jews and their Christian neighbors. On an overt level, there is a different Sabbath and some different holidays, and some Jews do observe dietary restrictions. There are also differences in historical traditions and in many cultural values. For some Jews, there are different religious traditions and guidelines. There is also an apparent oddity (at least odd to some) in the tendency of Jews to vote in a highly political liberal tradition despite relatively high levels of income. All of these differences contribute, along with the other factors mentioned here and Jews' historical status as outsiders in Western culture, to the continuing view of Jews as outsiders in the American society of the 1980s.

2
Jewish Americans and Entrepreneurial Occupations: A Success Story

> It did predispose them to independence and self-sufficiency since they lived in a hostile or indifferent society; . . . to progressive industries, where innovation was rewarded; and to peripheral industries, which allowed for expansion without direct competition with basic mainstream competition. Consequently, the Jewish entrepreneurial spirit and tradition of risk-taking has led them into the peripheral and the marginal, creative and novel areas of existence. (Krefetz, 1982, pp. 11–12)

On June 8, 1986, the *New York Times* published a special section on the world of business that included articles on some of our major entrepreneurial figures. Among the significant leaders who came in for special attention were two Americans of the Jewish faith, Lawrence Tisch and Leslie Wexner. Mr. Tisch, a native of Brooklyn, New York, has become one of the major U.S. figures in the world of finance, real estate, hotel management, and most recently, television. At the time of the article, Lawrence Tisch had just become the major stockholder of the Columbia Broadcasting System and was on his way to assuming active leadership of the company.

Leslie Wexner, a native of Columbus, Ohio, is a person of similar significance in the world of fashion retailing. During a period of two decades, he has built his company, The Limited, Inc., into a multidivisional retailing chain worth over a billion dollars. During this process, the management and marketing procedures used by Mr. Wexner have become, in the eyes of many, a model for the retailing industry.

The fame and success of Lawrence Tisch and Leslie Wexner are illustrative of the entrepreneurial and management contributions made by American Jews to the business community of this country. Although these men are clearly two of the more successful examples of such contributions, their achievements illustrate the great importance of the entrepreneurial role and entrepreneurial opportunities for Jewish Americans since our country was founded.

Why Entrepreneurial Careers? The Influence of Environmental Opportunity, Childhood Socialization, and the Outsider Factor

Several reasons can be cited in accounting for the attractiveness of entrepreneurial careers to members of the Jewish American community and for their success in such occupations. One factor has been the continuing receptivity of the American business setting to those who were willing and able to make entrepreneurial contributions.

> It was perhaps easiest for Jews in America to jettison the ancestral baggage of predetermined occupations, for the United States welcomed risk-taking and provided fertile ground for an open and competitive economy. The Jewish entrepreneurial spirit could find any number of outlets: though it made no frontal attack on the economic establishment it did take Jews into novel areas, businesses that were on the periphery of established industries and into areas of innovation where creative intuition counted for something. (Krefetz, 1982, p. 68)

The American culture into which the immigrants came in the late nineteenth and early twentieth centuries was booming and growing. There were dynamic changes almost every day, and there were few of the traditional cultural and religious constraints of Europe. The opportunities were there then (as they are there now) for those with the appropriate personal and social characteristics to make the entrepreneurial contributions that they wanted to make and that the American business setting needed.

Among the individuals and groups with the appropriate characteristics were those of the Jewish faith. Values such as deferring gratification and accepting responsibility for your own fate are values that Jews have traditionally taught their children, and they are also the values that predispose one to become interested in and successful at an entrepreneurial career (McClelland, 1961). One reason that Jews were both able and likely to develop and teach their children characteristics associated with development of entrepreneurial interests and competence is that their family life has typically included characteristics that encourage development of the ability to defer gratification and to control one's own fate—that is, a great degree of warmth, high achievement standards, and a low level of father dominance (father–child relationships not marked by authoritarian patterns).

Most important among these factors in understanding Jews' interest in entrepreneurial activities is that intrinsic to the Jewish faith is the belief that individuals must take responsibility for controlling their own lives and their own actions. Similarly, because Jews are not fatalists and believe that the world is susceptible to control, there is an acceptance of the principle of deferral of gratification (since they know that their rewards will eventually come if they are capable enough). In other words, rewards are under one's own control, not that of others; hence, one can defer gratification and call it up whenever one decides to do so.

> In Judaism, as the late Gershon Scholem wrote, "the Messianic idea has compelled a life lived in deferment." In contrast to the fatalism that characterized the culture of some other immigrant groups, Jews have always seen the world as susceptible to human control. In Jewish religious thought there is no divine jealousy of human activity and no inhibition against interfering with the forces of nature; on the contrary, God and man are viewed as partners in the work of creation. (Silberman, 1985, p. 136)

It is precisely these types of childhood socialization patterns and personal characteristics, which are characteristic of Jewish life, and that are needed for successful entrepreneurial activity.

Another important factor that made the entrepreneurial role particularly attractive to a group that was perceived as and perceived itself as an outsider in American life is that the role is essentially self-controlled. Traditionally wary of subjecting themselves to the control of other individuals and groups, Jews in this country have found the entrepreneurial role attractive because, in large part, "you are your own boss." Such freedom from the demands and evaluation of others had always been attractive to people who had learned over the years not to rely on others and who generally felt that they were outsiders in whatever nation they happened to be living in. These characteristics of high levels of self-control and independence have also accounted, in some part, for the attractiveness of the entrepreneurial role to Jews.

In sum, the entrepreneurial role became a success story for Jewish Americans because of the confluence of three factors. First, the American economy needed entrepreneurs to help it grow. Second, the childhood socialization patterns of Jews tended to encourage the traits and ways of looking at the world that lead one to look on entrepreneurial activities favorably. Third, the self-controlled nature of the entrepreneurial role made it particularly appealing to people who felt themselves to be outsiders and who therefore had to be wary about putting themselves under the influence and control of others.

Some Illustrations of Jews' Success in Entrepreneurial Careers

Systematic record-keeping of the kind that one finds in the professions is generally unavailable for entrepreneurs and entrepreneurial activity. Entrepreneurs are too individualistic, too competitive, and too busy starting and developing new ventures to be concerned with such matters. There are no recognized national professional associations for entrepreneurs, and there are no formalized professional training programs—such as one finds in medicine, law, and other professions—for becoming an entrepreneur. Anybody with sufficient capital and sufficient motivation to work can be an entrepreneur, a situation that is excellent for encouraging people to become entrepreneurs but does little to help in systematic record-keeping.

Therefore, although it is not easy to find systematic data on Jewish activity and/or success as entrepreneurs, considerable illustrative material is available regarding the extent and nature of the contributions made by Jews in various industries and settings. Such a review can provide us with some indication of the business interests that have often been found in the Jewish community, the skills and motivation that have been brought to bear on the challenges that are intrinsic to business enterprise, and the level of success that has been achieved.

Jewish Contributions to the Retailing, Entertainment, and Clothing/Fashion Industries

Of the major American industries, Jews have probably made their most prominent entrepreneurial contributions to the retailing, entertainment, and clothing/fashion industries. As we review such contributions, however, it is also important that we keep in mind that there have also been major contributions in each of these industries from non-Jewish people. As will be pointed out later, the so-called concept of a Jewish industry only means an industry in which there is a Jewish presence. It does *not* mean an industry that is dominated by a Jewish presence or that has even a majority of Jews.

Although they are highly diverse in nature, the retailing, entertainment, and clothing/fashion industries do have a common characteristic: they do not require major capital investments for start-up purposes. Products and services may be offered on either a large- or small scale basis in all of these industries, but the need for capital investment in the form of large-scale technical construction is not great. Thus, each of these industries and the Jewish activity in them have reflected an ages-old feeling among some Jews that they had best develop businesses and careers that were portable and could be taken along if one had to or wanted to leave. One type of "portable" career is one of the professions—medicine, law, and the like. Another is entrepreneurial activity in an industry with a low level of capital investment.

For illustrative purposes, we can cite in the retailing industry more than a dozen department stores/retailing chains that were originially founded by Jews and that, in some cases, are still controlled by the same families: Macy's, Gimbel's, Bloomingdale's, Rich's, Neiman-Marcus, Kauffman's, Sears and Roebuck, Abraham and Straus, B. Altman, Stern's, Saks, Loehmann's, Milton Petrie, and The Limited. Not all of these stores are still in existence; some are now part of larger chains; and in at least one case, the founding family is no longer Jewish. Taken as a group, however, they suggest the extent of the entrepreneurial and management contributions made by Jewish families to the retailing industry in this country.

Somewhat the same picture occurs when we look at the supermarket industry. Here, also, there are a significant number of Jewish-originated enterprises. Among the supermarkets that trace their origins to Jewish entrepreneurs are Stop-and-Shop (a New England chain), Waldbaums (New York and southern New England), Supermarkets General (New York), ShopRite (New Jersey), and Giant Foods (Washington, D.C., and surrounding states).

In many ways, the entertainment industry is very much like retailing in terms of the number and significance of the Jewish contributors. However, unlike the retailing industry, whose leaders have often been prominently identified with the Jewish community, the entertainment industry had, for many years, a different climate of opinion concerning Jewish affiliations. The movie industry, in particular, attempted for many years to minimize its Jewish image by, for example, requiring that its Jewish movie stars change their names to more Anglo-sounding names and by not making films that could in any way be connected with supporting Jewish causes or with reflecting any concern with Jewish problems, such as anti-Semitism in this country or the Holocaust during and after World War II. In some cases, the word was passed to employees that they were not to refer to the Jewish origins of the company leaders, and at least one major figure in the industry converted out of the religion before his death. Yet despite these attempts to repress any sense of Jewishness in the industry, the fact remains that Jews made major contributions to the creative, production, marketing, and financial aspects of the entertainment industry. Of particular significance here was the Hollywood movie industry, in which names such as Louis B. Mayer, Samuel Goldwyn, David O. Selznick, Adolph Zukor and the Warner Brothers were associated for decades with the entrepreneurial flair and creativity that made the name *Hollywood* synonymous with the word *glamour*. Similarly, when TV came along to take the limelight as the most important entertainment medium in history, there were Jews such as William Paley, Norman Lear, and David Sarnoff to assume leading entrepreneurial and eventually management roles in building the industry to the dominance it has today.

The clothing industry has traditionally been called a "Jewish industry." Stories and data are legend of the thousands of Jewish-owned firms, mostly small, that have been part of this industry since its development in the late nineteenth century. One reason for such Jewish presence in the industry is the previously noted significance of minimal capital investment needs. All that was required to be in business was a sewing machine and a place to put it—so long as one had imagination and the willingness and energy to go out and sell. As a result, the clothing industry served, in great part, as the mechanism for upward mobility for thousands of first-generation Jewish immigrants, both as workers and as entrepreneurs. Even today, the world of fashion and clothing has remained an industry in which the premium is on creativity, flexibility, and the ability to meet and respond to the needs of a constantly changing market. It is a world that has served as a good match to the needs and desires of many Jewish Americans, and they have responded—to the benefit of the American economy, the American society, the Jewish American community, and themselves.

Other Contributions of Jewish Entrepreneurs

The retailing, entertainment, and clothing/fashion industries have by no means been the only settings for major entrepreneurial contributions by Jews. In virtually any industry in which the need for capital construction funds was minimal—industries as varied as real estate/construction and publishing—Jews have developed and managed major enterprises and, sometimes, have contributed significant innovations in product development and marketing strategy. In real estate and construction, there have been major Jewish builders in San Francisco (Walter Shorenstein), Detroit (Philip and Max Stollman), New York (Samuel J. Lefrak), and Washington (Charles J. Smith). In some cases, Jewish entrepreneurs have built major national or worldwide enterprises. For example, Melvin Simon of Indianapolis is one of the major shopping center developers in this country, and the Pritzker family of Chicago has built the name Hyatt into one of the most famous names in the world in the hotel industry (as well as more recently moving into the airline industry with their purchase of Braniff Airways).

There are other examples, as well. Among the publishing enterprises originally owned by Jewish families are the *New York Times* and the Newhouse chain of newspapers; book and magazine publishers such as Simon and Schuster, Random House, and *TV Guide;* and such book clubs as the Book-of-the-Month Club and the Literary Guild. Jewish entrepreneurs have been involved in the development and marketing of yeast, yogurt, and other dairy products; in drugs and pharmaceuticals, both in the manufacturing and retailing phases; and even in the oil industry, an industry in which Jewish executives are virtually unknown today. Yet Amoco, one of the major giants of the industry, was founded by Edward Blaustein and was controlled for years by the Blaustein family. Similarly, the Amerada Hess company, a major distributor on the East Coast, is owned and controlled by the Hess family, and Occidental Petroleum is controlled by Dr. Armand Hammer. All of these individuals are Jewish. Similarly:

> Jewish business successes pop up in the most unexpected places: from whiskey (Edgar Bronfman of Seagram*) to birdseed (Leonard Stern of Hartz Mountain), from lipstick (Charles Revson of Revlon) to grain trading (Michel Fribourg of Continental Grain), from defense contracting (Henry Crown of General Dynamics) to floor coverings (Jesse Werner of GAF), from precious metals (the late Charles Engelhard of Engelhard Minerals and Chemicals) to dress patterns (James Schapiro of Simplicity Patterns), from temporary personnel agencies (the Scheinfelds and Winters of Man-

---

*The Bronfmans are a Canadian family but have made major entrepreneurial contributions in the United States. (Krefetz, 1982, p. 84)

power) to photocopying (Max Palevsky of Xerox), from computer hardware (Simon Ramo of TRW) to computer software (H. Taub and F. Lautenberg of Automatic Data Processing), and from hotels (the late Ben Swig of the Fairmount Hotel Chain) to cheese cake (Nathan Cummings of Consolidated Foods).

I could list more, but the point is well established. Success as entrepreneurs and the management of business organizations resulting from such success have been roles for which Jews have found themselves well suited in the United States, and they have contributed greatly for well over a century. In these occupations and careers, Jews' status as outsiders has had minimal negative impact, and their resulting achievements are a matter of record. It should always be kept in mind, however, that not all Jewish entrepreneurs have built major enterprises, nor have they all been successful in any sense of the word. As for any other group, the risks of entrepreneurial ventures have far more often resulted in failures than in successes. In the fashion industries, in retailing, and in any other business, the problems in starting up enterprises and keeping them going until the attainment of meaningful financial success are great. As a result, the entrepreneurial history of the Jews in the United States is far more dotted with failures than with successes. The successes we have noted here only illustrate what has been possible given the opportunity for economic contribution by Jews in America. They should in no way be interpreted as a claim that such contributions to the American society and economy were guaranteed.

3

Managerial/Executive Roles: The Implications of Outsider Status

T he attribution of outsider status to a job applicant has different implications for selection and other personnel decisions, depending on the job involved. Positions that involve extensive social interaction and a need for social acceptability are more likely to lead to problems for those viewed as outsiders than jobs that do not have such demands. Since social acceptability is particularly crucial in the performance of managerial and executive job demands, we would expect that the insider-outsider factor would be particularly important in selecting candidates for these positions and career paths. On the other hand, for positions and/or careers that do not particularly call for skills in social interaction, the insider-outsider factor would not be a critical component in the choices made; other types of personal requirements would most likely be used for selection and other types of personnel decisions. Typical of the latter jobs are staff/research and professional positions that call for specialized higher-level training—for example, law, accounting, computing.

In this and the next several chapters, we will see that this relationship between type of job demand and the resulting personnel decision making is crucial for understanding how the view of the Jews as outsiders in American life has affected the likelihood of Jews' being selected for managerial/executive roles in corporate America as contrasted to the likelihood of their being selected for professional positions and their engaging in professional career roles in general.

The Significance of Social Acceptability
in the Managerial/Executive Role

In and of itself, the lack of social acceptability should have little significance in the work setting—a setting that prides itself, supposedly, on rationality and "bottom-line" considerations. Yet social acceptability does have an important impact on managerial role performance; as a result, it does appear to have a negative impact on the likelihood of Jews' being hired for managerial and executive positions. The question is why social acceptability is perceived as important in the managerial-executive role.

One reason for the significance of social acceptability is that the manager's job is interactive. It involves attaining organizational goals through interactions with others. Sometimes these others may be subordinates, peers, and/or organizational superiors; sometimes they may be representatives of other organizations. In all of these cases, the process is similar, in that the tasks involve interactions and communication with others, and the effectiveness of such interactions depends in part on the accuracy with which each party can read and understand the other. The managerial job is inherently subjective; few objective role demands can be specifically keyed to the manager. The manager is free to interact in any way he or she wishes, but the logic is always the same—the attainment of organizational goals through others. It is because the managerial/executive role involves such ambiguity that selection for managerial positions relies so strongly on such elements as predictability and the degree to which the hiring supervisor could "feel comfortable" working with an individual. Jobs that are unpredictable and ambiguous can be understood (and supervised) best by making it as certain as possible that the person who occupies the role will act in a way that the responsible supervisor can understand, empathize with, and predict. If the person who occupies the role is not a person with whom the supervisor can feel comfortable, is not understandable, and is not predictable, how will the supervisor be able to know what is going on, and how will he or she be able to influence it? One way to achieve this sense of comfort and this understanding and predictability is to choose a person much like oneself (that is, one who is "inside" one's own group), since an insider is more predictable, easier to understand, and therefore easier to work with. On the other hand, an outsider is perceived as a person with whom it will be harder to feel comfortable and who will be more difficult to understand and predict—or so the person doing the hiring may think. This view of the Jewish applicant as a person who may think differently, who may have different values, and who will likely not provide the emotional warmth and predictability of a similar background and belief system appears to generate the reluctance to treat Jews equitably in selecting for managerial and executive positions.

Also adding to this tendency to favor the selection of insiders for managerial/executive positions is the importance of anxiety in what takes place in organizations. Work organizations must encourage some anxiety if they are to attain their goals. Organizations with no anxiety at all would contain only people who don't care about anything—hardly a promising prospect for the attainment of organizational objectives. Sometimes the anxiety is greater than at other times, and sometimes it is greater in some units of an organization than in others, but it is almost always present in some degree. This constancy is important to keep in mind in understanding how insiders and outsiders interact, because one of the most common effects of anxiety is the seeking out of friends and other means of social support who will help us reduce the anxiety. Managers and executives are no different from anyone else. When they are anxious—and they are usually very much at the center of organizationally linked anxiety—the presence of individuals with whom they feel comfortable can be very reassuring. Although it is hard to say how frequently the anxiety factor influences the desire to hire someone for a managerial position with whom one can feel comfortable, the pervasiveness of anxiety in organizational processes suggests that it may at times have significant impact on such decisions.

The Impact of the Outsider Factor on Jewish Managers: Findings from Empirical Research

The Ohio State Study

Perhaps the most comprehensive research ever conducted in the United States on how being Jewish influences the likelihood of being treated equitably in executive selection and promotion was the study conducted at Ohio State University by Powell (1969). Although the data were collected sometime during the mid-1960s and should be looked at with this limitation, Powell's findings continue to provide valuable insights into the impact of the view of the Jews as outsiders on the likelihood that they will be able to attain successful managerial/executive careers.

The methodology Powell followed in his investigation consisted of four separate phases and indicates a high degree of carefulness in his research. Phase 1 consisted of participant observation in two firms over a period of five years. This was then followed by phases involving confidential information gathering from a variety of individuals in different companies and industries and the conducting of in-depth interviews with community leaders in major social clubs in two metropolitan areas. Following these stages, the final phase of the research involved interviews and administration of questionnaires to 263 middle- to upper-level executives from a wide range of industries, from whom 239 usable responses were eventually obtained.

Significant among the findings reported by Powell was the openness with which the executives admitted that being a member of the Jewish faith negatively influenced the possibility of a successful career as an organizational executive. Table 3–1 summarizes some of these findings regarding the degree to which being Jewish was viewed as hindering an executive career in general or one's perceived specific promotability (compared to being a member of some other religion). It is clear from the data that being a member of the Jewish faith was seen as being a greater hindrance than any other type of religious-group membership.

What reasons were given for the hindering effect of being Jewish on one's executive career? Powell's data indicate that the view of Jews as outsiders is a key factor. This can be seen in table 3–2, which lists the reasons for such views among executives and managers. As can be seen, each of the factors cited is a variant of the traditional perceptions of Jews as outsiders and as different from the so-called mainstream (for example, the historical tradition that viewed Jews as outsiders and as not trustworthy, "clannish," and not "socially acceptable").

Table 3–1
Summary of Findings: Perceived Impact of Being Jewish on an Executive Career, Compared to Other Religious Groups

(percentages)

Religious Group	General Impact		Impact on Promotability	
	Helps	Hinders	Helps	Hinders
Baptist	3.3	1.3	31.2	8.3
Episcopal	3.8	0.4	43.1	1.8
Congregational	3.3	0.4	35.8	3.7
Methodist	3.3	0.4	36.7	1.8
Lutheran	3.8	0.4	34.9	2.8
Presbyterian	4.2	0.4	42.2	1.8
Roman Catholic	5.4	2.5	28.4	20.2
Mormon	6.7	2.1	30.3	23.9
Jewish	0.4	23.4	8.3	63.3
Agnostic	—	—	5.5	39.4

Source: R. M. Powell, *Race, Religion and the Promotion of the American Executive* (Columbus: College of Administrate Science, The Ohio State University, 1969), pp. 67, 107, 109.

Table 3–2
Reasons for the Hindering Influence of Being Jewish on Executive Promotability

Reason	Percentage Citing Reason
Traditional public prejudice toward group	10.1
Feelings of distrust	9.2
Tendency toward group conscientiousness and clannishness—no fellowship with majority group	7.3
Stereotypical negative image, except for Jewish industries	5.5
Fear of customer prejudice or negative public relations	3.7
Group not socially accepted in company	2.8

Source: R. M. Powell, *Race, Religion and the Promotion of the American Executive* (Columbus: College of Administrate Science, The Ohio State University, 1969), p. 118.

Further support for the significance of the outsider factor's negative impact on the likelihood of success in a managerial/executive career is provided in another part of Powell's research, in which he attempted to determine the specific areas in which the respondents believed that being Jewish would help in performing the managerial role and the areas in which it might hinder performance. According to these results, the executives believed that being Jewish would be of great value in aspects of the job that call for managerial capability, intellectual curiosity, ethics and moral scruples, ambition and drive, and self-reliance. However, consistent with the view of Jews as outsiders, they also believed that being Jewish would hinder an executive greatly in social aspects of the job, such as developing necessary friendships inside and outside the firm and interacting effectively with others. Consistent with this was the finding that executives who had succeeded socially on the job by becoming a member of an important social club were more pessimistic about the ability of Jews to succeed as executives than those who had not joined a social club (although both were highly pessimistic).

The Michigan Study

The outsider explanation for the relative absence of Jews from executive and managerial roles in much of corporate America is also supported in an independent, smaller-scale investigation, also conducted in the mid-1960s but at the University of Michigan Institute for Social Research (Quinn, Kahn, Tabor, and Gordon, 1968). Basically a questionnaire simulation study of the potential role of anti-Semitism in the selection of candidates for managerial positions, this investigation focused on managers and executives from a group of companies in the Cleveland-Akron area that enjoyed a reputation of being relatively "open" to Jews at the time the research was conducted. Of the 139 individuals in the sample, half were no more than two levels below the president; as a group, they represented most of the functional areas of management.

As in the Powell study, a major finding in the Michigan research was the high degree of openness with which discrimination against Jews was reported. For example, 23 percent of the sample agreed with the statement "anyone who employs many people should be careful not to hire a large percentage of Jews," and 19 percent agreed with the statement "I probably would not choose a Jewish person for promotion if an equally qualified non-Jew were available." Both of these responses reflect concrete actions, and the figures would seem to be rather high for companies that were supposedly relatively open to Jews. On the other hand, only 6 percent agreed with the more abstract statement "In general, I am reluctant to hire or promote Jewish people into important management positions," and nobody disagreed with the statement "Jewish persons should be hired or promoted on the same basis as everyone." Thus, an important finding of this investigation was that the expression of direct, openly anti-Semitic attitudes was more likely under concretely stated conditions than under abstract ones.

There is also research support in this study regarding the importance of the view of Jews as outsiders in influencing the manner in which executive and managerial selection and promotion decisions take place. In one analysis, 47 percent of the managers who were inclined to discriminate against Jews tended to agree with the statement "Most of the time you can tell a person is Jewish by his physical appearance," as compared to 20 percent of the managers who were not inclined to discriminate. In another analysis, it was found that the group with the strongest inclination to discriminate against Jews (75 percent) were those who felt that the social credentials of Jews were poor and that social credentials were important for the managerial role. Those groups that felt either that Jews had good social credentials or that social credentials were unimportant were less likely to discriminate. For them, the inclination to discriminate ranged from 18 percent to 39 percent.

Recent Investigations of Jews as Outsiders in Corporate America

Research investigations since the work of Powell and Quinn have continued to find that the view of Jews as lacking social acceptability and the view of them as outsiders in American corporate life are rather common and that such views are frequently cited as reasons for negatively assessing their acceptability for promotion to higher levels of management. One body of research that supports this argument is the studies that have focused on country club membership, traditionally viewed as of significant importance in determining the acceptability of individuals for executive roles:

> Of the more than 4,000 Jews whose corporate and club affiliations they traced, only 24 belonged to one or more of the country's top level clubs. In one study, which matched a group of Jewish philanthropists with a group of Gentile philanthropists, the non-Jews were four times more likely to be members of such clubs. . . . In addition, the researchers surveyed many of the top city clubs around the country to see if they accepted Jewish members. They found that, as of the late 1970's, the Chicago Club was estimated to have between six and fifteen Jewish members; the Detroit Club at least six; Los Angeles' California Club between one and three; and Seattle's Rainier Club between six and eight Jewish members. Seven clubs were thought to have no Jewish members: Atlanta's Piedmont Driving Club; Chicago's Casino Club; Houston's Eagle Lake; Milwaukee's Milwaukee Club; Philadelphia's Philadelphia Club; Pittsburgh's Rolling Rock; and St. Louis' St. Louis Country Club. (Zweigenhaft, 1984, p. 8)

The unwillingness to accept Jews as club members provides additional evidence that Jews are often seen as not socially acceptable and as outsiders in corporate life. Although some have argued that the significance of such club memberships may have lessened in recent years and that perhaps a few more clubs now accept Jews as members (and the opinions on both of these questions are mixed), the very existence of clubs as mechanisms for executive selection suggests the importance of the social acceptability factor in affecting the likelihood of success as an executive in organizational settings and the perceived inappropriateness of Jews for such roles. Also involved here may be a "Catch 22" phenomenon, whereby Jews are not admitted to such clubs because of their lack of social acceptability and then such lack of membership is cited as an indication of the inappropriateness of Jewish applicants for executive roles.

Also consistent with this reasoning is a study undertaken in the early 1980s of MBA graduates of the Harvard Business School

(Zweigenhaft, 1984). This study found that being socially compatible and fitting in to the company continue to be important in hiring and promotion practices. According to the respondents in this study, it did not matter whether or not such a requirement is bigoted. The fact is that social acceptability criteria are important in furthering one's career; these criteria are used, and those perceived as outsiders have this barrier to cross (p. 11). Consistent with this were the other findings of the research—that being viewed as "too Jewish" and "too visible as a Jew" continues to hurt in corporate upward mobility (p. 14) and that wearing a yarmulke (skullcap) would definitely hurt in the corporate setting. Overall, the findings of this investigation of Harvard MBAs suggest that if Jews are to succeed at executive levels in most corporations, they will have to be Jews with few outward signs of Jewish identity (for example, dietary preferences, Sabbath observance, and the wearing of a yarmulke) and also with little interest in activities outside the corporate world that signify interest in the problems of Jewish life in contemporary America (for example, an interest in the state of Israel or the problems of Soviet Jewry).

A note of caution is necessary here, however. The design of this last study was problematic in several ways. One problem is that the sample finally obtained was quite small and was probably not very representative of the original target population, since secondary recommendations from original respondents for classmates who could be surveyed were utilized, probably in a nonsystematic manner. A second problem is that the group assessed is a rather unique one—that is, graduates of one of the most prestigious business schools in America, one that is virtually certain to open doors to corporate America. However, the data do include recent observations of the conditions of organizational life for Jews by a knowledgeable group of individuals. For this reason alone, they do need to be attended to.

Further Evidence for the Outsider Hypothesis: An Interview Study of the Role of Jews in Corporate America

To gain further clarification of some of the factors that enter into the more contemporary decision-making patterns of higher-level corporate executives regarding the recruitment and employment of Jews—and, in particular, the impact of their possible outsider characteristics on such decisions—I conducted a series of interviews with two groups of individuals. The first group consisted of eleven management consultants, Jewish and non-Jewish, in the general areas of leadership, organizational and executive development, and human resource management. All but two of the interviewees had doctorates in psychology. Their experience ranged from ten to thirty years' work with the highest levels of corporate executives in Fortune 500 and Fortune Service 500 organizations, and at the time of the interviews, all were quite successful in their consulting practice. Of particular relevance to us here is that each of the individuals had long had personal access to both CEOs and higher-level executives and were quite familiar with the attitudes, motivations, and cognitive processes of these executives.

The second group interviewed consisted of fourteen managers, Jewish and non-Jewish, in both the public and private sectors. Their organizational level ranged from middle to upper ranks, and they came from a mixed group of organizations in terms of Jewish representation at the executive level.

The general purpose of the interviews was to focus on the interviewees' perceptions of the general position of Jews in contemporary corporate America and how that position might have changed over the years. Though essentially unstructured, the interviews were designed to include such topics as the presence of Jews in higher-level management in industries and companies with which the interviewees were familiar, the possible changes (if any) that had taken place over the years, the reasons they saw for a Jewish presence or lack of it, the possible explanations for their observations, and their beliefs regarding what might happen in the foreseeable future. Because of the small number of interviews conducted, no effort was made to analyze the data quantitatively. Instead, the analysis involved coding and classifying the major themes emerging from the interviews. It is these themes that will be reported here.

Theme 1: None of the interviewees expressed any surprise at the lack of a significant Jewish presence at the senior executive level of major American corporations.

In general, the interviewees expressed the belief that any other result would have been open to considerable question on their part. To quote one consultant:

> I don't know where Jews ever got the idea that they had it made in corporations. My experience is that this is simply not so, and I don't believe anyone who is familiar with American corporations would think any differently.

The lack of Jews at any significant managerial/executive level was particularly unsurprising to those interviewees whose experience had been primarily in the oil industry. One consultant, a former manager in one of the largest of the oil giants, said:

> I would question any results that would have been any different from these. There is little doubt in my mind that Jews have been systematically excluded from senior executive levels in most oil companies.

Similarly, according to another consultant with extensive experience in the oil industry:

> There was no question about it. When we sent people to any of the Arab countries, they made it clear to us that they did not want to deal with any Jews. They also said the same things when they came here. They did not want to have anything to do with Jewish executives or managers.

The major differences between the consultants and the managers interviewed were that the Jewish managers were more forceful in stressing overt anti-Semitism as a basis for decision making. Several managers cited specific instances of such acts during their careers, which had affected them or other Jews in the organizations for which they worked. One manager quoted his supervisor as follows:

> "Now it's our turn. It's too bad if some of you get hurt, but that's your problem. I'm not looking for any Jews here. I'm not recruiting them, I'm not hiring them, and I'm not promoting them."

In contrast, most of the consultants believed the lack of Jewish presence was not always a reflection of conscious intent but could, in some cases, be reflecting a rarely thought about habitual pattern in organizations. According to them, there was reason to think (from their experience) that the lack of Jews at the more important managerial and executive levels might be reflecting the belief, right or wrong, that Jews were not interested in corporate employment— so there was no reason to attempt to recruit them.

> *Theme 2:* Jews who are hired into corporate settings learn quickly that in order to succeed, they will have to give up many of the symbolic behaviors that tie them to their Jewish heritage, regardless of the relevance of such behaviors to their job requirements.

The consultants and the managers agreed that those few Jews who have made it to the executive level in corporations that do not have Jewish family origins are almost all individuals who take little interest in affairs or concerns of the Jewish community. Virtually all interviewees said that a key requirement for success in these corporations is that individuals believe that their religious identity as Jews is something to be kept out of the public eye. One consultant with long experience in high-level consultation said that few successful corporate Jews appear to have any religious interest, nor are they involved in such concerns of the Jewish American community as Soviet Jewry or the problems of the state of Israel. In addition, according to this consultant, a noticeable pattern of aspiring Jewish executives was their attempt to exhibit speech and dress patterns that were as similar as possible to those of their non-Jewish colleagues:

> These guys are like vanilla. They have worked hard to get rid of any possible sign that they believe stamps them as Jewish. They dress and talk like stereotypes of their view of the Ivy League WASP. Sometimes, when you talk to them, you think you're watching a movie.

Of particular significance as a symbol to be avoided is the yarmulke, or skullcap, often worn by religious Jewish males. Despite its apparent lack of significance to job performance, the wearing of a skullcap apparently serves as a symbol of outsider status that is rarely, if ever, accepted in corporate life as appropriate for those aspiring to executive careers. One Jewish middle-level manager who wore such a skullcap told of the frequent difficulties he and others he knew had had as a result, both in the company he worked for and in previous years of job-seeking:

> When I was looking for a job, they told me not to wear it. But I did anyway. I decided that if this piece of cloth could make them so antagonistic, then the hell with them. This piece of cloth could do nothing to them, yet they acted as if it would. I decided that I wouldn't take it off but that I would do the best job I could, even though it might hurt me eventually, and it probably has.

It might be noted that some Jewish executives found these constraints on the expression of their identity perfectly acceptable and in keeping with their own attitudes; others saw them as unreasonable. Unreasonable or not, however, the interviewees were unanimous in viewing them as integral parts of the corporate landscape.

Theme 3: The absence of Jews in much of corporate America and the expectation that Jews who are hired give up part of their symbolic heritage, regardless of job relevance, is generally viewed as permissible and understandable behavior in corporate America, since there are few systematic, continuing complaints from the Jewish community about such corporate expectations.

Most of the consultants interviewed took special pains to point out how sensitive corporate executives are to protests from consumer and other advocate groups and how little public pressure there has been in this particular area concerning corporate selection and promotion practices. As several consultants indicated, one only has to look at the gains that women have made in recent years in levels and types of employment to cite the values of public protest.

Yet both the consultants and the managers emphasized, the latter with much more anger, that there has been little such protest from the American Jewish community. As one manager said rather heatedly:

> I wonder if they believe that things happen just like this. To expect business corporations to make changes on their own without any protest and without any pressure is totally naive and indicates how little they understand the world of business.

Theme 4: Jews are often considered as candidates for professional/staff positions but are discouraged in a number of ways from considering themselves candidates for executive career paths, even though many Jewish professionals may have such aspirations.

A pattern that showed up continually in the interviews was that Jews were present in a variety of staff/professional positions in companies where they were virtually totally absent from higher-level managerial/executive roles. One interviewee remarked that there were a number of Jews in his company in professional jobs but that he was the only Jew in a managerial role at his level, a third-level position, and that he had no expectations of going any higher. In another interview at an engineering firm, a Jewish personnel executive said:

> There are plenty of Jewish engineers in this company, but none are project managers, nor will there be any so far as I know. I believe that most of them have been told informally that the company is happy to have them as engineers but that our customers are unwilling to work with Jewish executives.

It was this interviewee's belief that the position taken by the company regarding the desires of customers was probably a rationalization for its own attitudes concerning the roles it expected or would allow Jews to play in the company, but he had never tested this belief by actual questioning of the individuals involved.

Another way in which those who were Jewish were sometimes reminded of their outsider status was to be denied job titles appropriate to their responsibilities, particularly when such titles involved perceived executive status. In one case, the interviewee pointed out that according to the organization chart, a Jewish manager in the firm should have had the title executive vice-president, but he had not been given that title. The reason, according to the individual involved, was that "he didn't go to the right church." In another case in which a Jewish manager did not have a job title that was traditional in the company for his level of responsibilities, the individual involved strongly believed that his religion was the reason. He believed that one reason the reluctance had occurred was that the relevant job title would have made him a corporate officer, and that division had never had a Jewish corporate officer.

An important theme in some interviews was that the availability of professional/staff positions for Jews does not in any way decrease the frustration that is felt because of the lack of opportunity to pursue managerial/executive career paths. Increasingly, as several of the interviewees pointed out, Jews who are looking to make mid-career changes from professional to managerial positions are finding their paths blocked and are forced to stay where they are because of the corporate lack of willingness to hire Jews for the managerial positions. Also adding to their frustration is the increased hiring of minority group members as the result of direct and indirect pressures from government agencies and civil rights groups. The managers pointed out that the managerial and executive career path positions are remaining closed to them; as a result, some of them are staying in "stereotypical" professional careers that they no longer want or desire, if indeed they ever really did.

4
Jews and Corporate America: From Post–World War I to the Mid-1970s

The status of Jews as outsiders in corporate America has affected their levels and types of careers and employment from the days when Jews were the predominant group on New York's Lower East Side and they began to make their movement upward. Although it became increasingly evident during the period between the two world wars that Jews were overcoming strong patterns of exclusion to attain economic and social success in the professions and in the world of entrepreneurial opportunities, their absence from major segments of the corporate world during this period of growth was apparent to all who looked. Perhaps even more significant is that the same patterns have continued to the present.

Patterns of Jewish Employment in Corporate America: 1918–41

By the end of World War I, most of the major occupational, industrial, and organizational structures that were to characterize our economy for the next fifty years had begun to assume shape. It was during this era that the large manufacturing and production-oriented corporations began to dominate American life, a dominance that has remained to the present, even as they have had to share their influence with the increasing presence of service organizations. It was also during this era that an employment pattern developed for Jews in this country that has not changed significantly to the present, well over a half-century later.

During the decade of the 1920's, they [Jews] were largely closed out from those industrial companies which controlled more than half of corporate wealth and perhaps 35 to 45 percent of total business wealth. Nor were they readily admitted to such basic sectors of the economy as commercial banking, insurance and public utilities. They were left to practice free enterprise, if they could, in soft goods, retail trade, the amusement industry, communications, and some marginal industries with large risk factors. Even in the retail field, the local store might be Jewish-owned; the chain store was not.

Jewish entrepreneurial skills in the fields that were open to them, nevertheless, produced successes that in time created a considerable economic upper class and a prosperous middle class. Yet, the growing concentration of industry in large corporate enterprises depressed the employment opportunities of young Jewish men and women to whom even low-level clerical jobs were closed off. . . .

A mass of empirical evidence pointed to the difficulty Jews faced in getting even the lowliest jobs in the corporate world. The want-ad sections of newspapers in cities such as New York and Philadelphia frankly acknowledged the resistance to Jewish job seekers. Even when newspapers refused to print the blunt phrasing "no Jews need apply," applicants could be asked to "state race and religion" or be denied consideration when interviewed. . . .

A survey of 21 commercial employment agencies in June 1929 by the Bureau of Jewish Social Research came up with some telling figures. One refused to register Jews and another said it could place no Jews. Eight were discouraging because they thought their efforts would be an exercise in futility. Seven were willing to chance an effort to place Jewish clerical workers, and only six said that they could find jobs for Jewish girls.

The Vocational Service for Juniors, a New York East Side voluntary agency seeking jobs for young people, reviewing ten years of effort, reported finding 12,000 jobs for its 27,000 applicants. Half of these applicants were Catholic, 30 percent Protestant and 38 percent Jewish. Thus, 44 percent of all applicants were placed, but only 20 percent of the Jewish applicants found employment, even though they were often better qualified.

At a higher level of job seeking, Broun and Britt reported figures from the alumni employment agency of a major university, where 15 percent of the graduating class was Jewish. Three months after commencement, as a routine matter, those without jobs were referred to the bureau. Of those still unplaced, 40 percent were Jews. (Belth, 1979, pp. 111–12)

The employment patterns of American Jews during the two decades prior to World War II are well described by the foregoing quotation. Among these patterns were the following:

1. Jews were not employed to any meaningful extent in our major industrial corporations—that is, those that controlled an overwhelming portion of our nation's wealth and employed a major proportion of our working population.

2. Jews had difficulty gaining employment in such industries as commercial banking, public utilities, and insurance.

3. Jews were being directed—both explicitly and, sometimes, more subtly—into entrepreneurial opportunities and more high-risk industries such as retailing, amusements, and soft goods.

4. In some instances, employment agencies were serving as screening mechanisms for employers that did not wish to hire Jews.

5. Even with other factors held equal—for example, graduation from the same college—Jews were finding it harder to gain employment than non-Jews with the same background.

One indication of some of the characteristic attitudes of corporate America toward Jews during this era, which may help in explaining the existence of these patterns, is suggested by the activities of Henry Ford, possibly the most important businessman in the United States during these years. In 1920, Henry Ford stood at the

very peak of American business. His development of the mass production lines from which his Model T automobiles poured forth
had made his name a synonym for a society in transformation. He
was, in the value system of the era, at the very peak of American
society.

It was at this time that Ford began to support a newspaper, the
Dearborn Independent, which for the next seven years was a symbol and rallying point for American anti-Semitism and anti-Semites.
Lies, distortions, and wild attacks on Jews and Judaism were common features of the *Dearborn Independent* during the time of Ford's
support. Among the material published by the newspaper during
these years was *The Protocols of the Elders of Zion,* a notorious
anti-Semitic forgery developed by the agents of the czar in the nineteenth century to justify their pogroms. There were also claims of
Jewish control of banks, a claim demonstrably false then and demonstrably false today, and such wild charges as the claims that Bene-
dict Arnold was a front for Jewish bankers and that Queen Isabella
of Spain, under whose reign the Spanish Inquisition began, was really a Jewish front. There were also charges that Jews were infiltrat-
ing the Jesuits. These claims, and others like them, were part of the
Dearborn Independent for the seven years that Ford supported the
newspaper, both financially and morally.

The importance of Ford's support for this publication is difficult
to overestimate, for Ford's prestige at the time was enormous. His
sanctioning of such virulent anti-Semitism very likely served to legitimate and support similar anti-Semitism among others in the
business world, and it certainly needs to be considered as a possible
factor in explaining the employment patterns we have noted. Ford
eventually ended his support of the newspaper, partially as a result
of legal problems and public pressures, and issued a public apology.
However, despite his withdrawal of support and his apology, Henry
Ford retained a negative image for the rest of his life, as least as far
as the American Jewish community was concerned.

Little changed in the 1930s from the picture described for the
previous decade. Although the involvement of Jews in the professions and in the business world as entrepreneurs continued to increase, despite barriers in the professional schools and in many colleges, their presence in the corporate world, particularly in

managerial roles, remained minimal. There was little movement toward any change for the better, as a result of the depressed economic conditions of the time and the considerable number of American fascist movements, which used American concerns about the situation in Europe to fan whatever anti-Semitic sentiment they could. The best that most Jews in America could hope for at the time was to hold on, as other Americans did, to whatever gains they had made during the previous decades and to live with the discrimination in the professions and in the colleges—and this is pretty much what they did.

Patterns of Jewish Employment in Corporate America: From World War II to the Mid-1970s

One of the frequent results of nightmarish events is that they often raise one's consciousness about the significance of such happenings. At least among well-meaning people, there is often an increased effort to understand what took place and to look for ways in which such events might be prevented in the future. So it was with the Holocaust. Unquestionably, the horror of the event had a major impact on much of mankind, and there were reactions on economic, social, and psychological levels.

One reaction here in the United States was an increased interest in the problem of anti-Semitism in the work setting. During the three decades immediately following World War II, there were a number of field investigations of discrimination against Jews in various employment contexts. However, despite their intent and their goals, these studies were really of two types, only one of which could be considered to be concerned with discrimination. This type included the actual studies of explicit anti-Semitism in employment-related decision making. The other, more typical investigations during this era were not so much studies of discrimination as frequency counts of the number of Jews in different industries—counts that might be a function of a number of other factors besides actual discriminatory decision making. Yet although these latter studies did not provide direct evidence that anti-Semitism was responsible for the patterns observed, they did prove to be useful in providing information concerning the occupational and career patterns of Jews in relation to corporate America during those years. Most important, these studies showed clearly that at a time when Jews were achieving high levels of success as entrepreneurs and as professionals, they remained absent, for the most part, from managerial and executive positions in much of corporate America.

Studies Documenting Anti-Semitism in Employment

During the 1950s, the Anti-Defamation League (ADL) of B'nai B'rith reported several studies of placement orders with public and private employment agencies and their resulting referral practices. Each documented widespread practices of conscious discrimination against Jews (Waldman, 1956).

The first of these investigations analyzed job orders placed with the Los Angeles offices of the California Public Employment Service. The study found that fully 50 percent of the management and professional orders and 27 percent of the requests for clerical employees discriminated against Jews. These figures are impressive on two counts. First, there is the absolute level of the percentages involved. Six years after the end of World War II, we find that fully one-half of the job orders for managerial and professional employees in one of the most important American cities consciously discriminated against Jews. Another reason for being impressed with these findings is that it is also probable that these figures, high as they are, may still be lower-bound estimates of the actual degree of anti-Semitic discrimination existing at the time. The reason for this is that people are probably less likely to report antisocial behavior on their part (such as discriminatory selection procedures) to a public agency than they would be to a private firm without public responsibilities. In support of this point, another of the ADL studies, conducted in 1955, also in California, found that 125 of 129 private agencies accepted job orders with discriminatory specifications (*Rights,* June, 1967).

Such high levels of anti-Semitic discrimination were not unique to California. Biased hiring procedures against Jews were common in both public and private employment agencies in many cities throughout the country. A 1953 ADL study in Chicago found that

27 percent of the job orders were discriminatory (Waldman, 1956), and a 1964 study found acceptance of discriminatory requests by thirty-two of thirty-four employment agencies in Phoenix and forty-one of forty-two in Atlanta (*Rights,* June, 1967). In the same vein, another ADL study during that era showed that acceptance rates of discriminatory orders among private employment agencies were 95 percent in Chicago (101 of 106), 95 percent in Kansas City (49 of 55), 85 percent in Los Angeles (66 of 77), 100 percent in Miami (38 of 38), 67 percent in New York (60 of 91), and 100 percent in Omaha (14 of 14) (ADL Bulletin, 1967). Also showing support for this general pattern of findings was a 1955 quasi field experiment by the American Jewish Congress in which 222 New York City agencies were called in order to place an ad for a white Protestant stenographer; 70.3 percent accepted the order, a figure that is generally consistent with the rates of acceptance for similar discriminatory placement requests in similar studies in 1946 (88.4 percent), 1948 (64. 2 percent), and 1952 (65 percent), (cited in Slavin and Pradt, 1982, pg. 94).

In sum, it seems clear that as a result of such a high frequency of discriminatory requests in job placement orders *and* a similarly high frequency of acceptance of such orders by public and private employment agencies, we can conclude that conscious anti-Semitic discrimination in employment practices was rather common during these years, and not just at managerial/executive levels.

Studies of Industry Employment Patterns

As mentioned earlier, studies of the extent and level of Jewish employment in different industries were also common during this era. Although these investigations provided little information about the conscious or unconscious intent of those responsible for personnel decisions in these contexts, the patterns depicted did show, conclusively, the lack of a Jewish presence in corporate America at a time when Jews were making major advances in entrepreneurial roles and in the professions.

Patterns in Commercial Banking. Commercial banks are among the major financial institutions of our society. They supply the financial fuel for our corporations and for our governments by lend-

ing funds for growth, for development, and for sundry other activities. Through their financial power and their activities, commercial
banks such as Citibank of New York, the Bank of America in California, and the Chase Manhattan Bank have become instantly recognized institutions worldwide. Of interest for us here is that despite the traditional claims of anti-Semitic demagogues from the
political right and political left concerning "Jewish bankers," it has
been true historically and remains so today that commercial banking as an industry is notable for its lack of Jewish executives. This
was true during the 1920s and 1930s; it was true during the 1950s,
1960s, and early 1970s; and it is still true for the most part today
(although there have been one or two signs of possible changes for
the better in the past few years).

Most of the evidence supporting this conclusion for the three
decades immediately following World War II comes from a series
of studies of the commercial banking industry, begun in 1960 by
the American Jewish Committee and continuing to this day in Philadelphia. The findings of the earlier studies (that is, in the 1960s and
1970s) may be summarized as follows (American Jewish Committee, 1967):

1. In 1960, a study of six leading commercial banks in Philadelphia showed that 12 of 1,216 executives (1 percent) were Jewish. Approximately 15 percent of the total Philadelphia population
at the time of the study was Jewish, and the percentage of Jewish
college graduates was even greater.

2. In 1966, a survey of the percentage of Jews at the senior and
middle management level in nine banks in the District of Columbia
found that 1 of 152 senior executives and 2 of 281 middle managers
were Jewish (.7% in both cases). Also reported in the same study
was a survey of nine banks in the New York area, which found that
1 of 173 senior executives (.7 percent) and 9 of 927 of the middle-
line managers (1 percent) were Jewish. During these years, approximately 10 percent of the District and 25 percent of the New York
area populations were Jewish, and the percentage of Jewish college
graduates in both cases was even greater.

3. Also in 1966, the American Jewish Committee found in a
nationwide survey of the fifty leading commercial banks that 8 of

632 senior executives (1.3 percent) were Jewish; the comparable figure for junior executives was 32 of 3,438 (.9 percent).

Patterns in the Insurance Industry. Like commercial banking, the insurance industry consists in great degree of large organizations with enormous financial resources that are invested in projects of significance to the business life of our nation and of the world. Because of the importance of this industry and its status as a large employer, the employment practices of insurance companies also came under examination by Jewish agencies during the 1950s and 1960s.

One question of interest was the proportion of Jewish employees in a particular company and their presence at different occupational levels. A second question, which was more specific to the insurance industry, referred to the possible differential placement of Jews in home or sales offices. This latter question was a particularly important consideration because of the way insurance was sold during these years. Although real decision-making power rested almost invariably in the home offices of the large insurance firms, most companies maintained large numbers of sales offices from which their representatives sold insurance to the people in the respective communities. Given these structural considerations of the industry, it was logical to think that an insurance company would select for a particular sales office those who would be most likely to meet the emotional and attitudinal characteristics of a community. At the same time, however, it was suspected that they would also select for home-office positions (that is, those to whom they might eventually wish to give major decision-making power) those who would be most acceptable for those roles according to the major attitudinal characteristics of the company. Stated in terms of the outsider hypothesis, the Jewish agencies conducting these investigations were concerned that Jews would be most likely to be hired where they would be socially acceptable—that is, in sales offices located in communities where there were Jews—and least likely to be hired where they supposedly would not be socially acceptable—that is, in the home office, where there was also the greatest opportunity for professional growth. Also, as part of the discriminatory process, these same research investigators thought that Jewish job applicants would not be selected for sales positions in communities where there were few Jews. Studies by the Anti-Defamation League during these years (*Rights*, 1959) showed that the selection and promotion patterns of the insurance industry did, indeed, conform to these predicted differences in hiring patterns between the home and sales offices. The research showed the following:

1. Of a total of 6,066 executives on the staffs of seven nation-wide insurance firms, 327 (5.4 percent) were Jewish. Since it was estimated at the time that Jews constituted approximately 7 percent of the total white-collar labor force in this country and about 9 percent of the college graduate labor force, this figure for the over-all level of Jewish employment in the insurance industry was a relatively positive one, particularly when compared to the figures for commercial banking.

2. This positive appraisal was somewhat misleading, however, since the findings did show the expected differences in Jewish employment levels in the home versus sales offices. In fact, whereas 3.6 percent of the executives in the home offices were Jewish and the figure for the sales offices was 6.2 percent, the discrepancy was even greater when other factors were considered. In the Greater New York area, the most heavily Jewish area in the United States, 10 percent of the sales office executives were Jewish, as compared to only 4.1 percent in the home offices of the companies. In fact, 200 (over 60 percent) of the total 327 Jewish executives were located in the New York area, primarily in sales offices. Nationwide, 236 of the 254 Jewish executives (approximately 93 percent) working in sales offices, had job titles that clearly indicated a sales focus to the position, as contrasted to 74 percent of non-Jews working in the sales offices. This was not accidental, and it supports the reasoning that has been presented, as pointed out in the report:

> 77 percent of all Jewish executives are to be found in four states—New York, New Jersey, Pennsylvania and Illinois. . . . This concentration of Jewish executives, mostly in sales functions, in four states with extremely large Jewish populations is not, according to well-informed sources, the result of happenstance. It flows, they say, from a design on the part of companies to hire and place

Jewish personnel usually in those areas where the absence of Jewish personnel might have public relations connotations, and where it is calculated that Jewish personnel can enhance the amount of insurance sold to Jews. The point is borne out when one examines the numbers of Jewish executives in communities with Jewish populations smaller than those found in the four above-mentioned states. Thus, in St. Louis, which has a Jewish population of 55,000, out of 34 executives employed by the insurance companies, only one was Jewish; in the twin cities of St. Paul and Minneapolis, with a combined Jewish population of 33,000, one out of 50 executives was Jewish; in Denver, with a Jewish population of 18,000, there were no Jews among the 31 executives; and in Indianapolis, with 8,000 Jews, there were no Jews among the 23 executives. (*Rights*, 1959, p. 61)

3. Even when Jewish executives were placed in home offices, there seems to have been a pattern—consistent with the view of Jews as outsiders—of placing them in professional staff, "brainy" positions, rather than in positions wielding executive decision-making power and calling for social acceptability within the higher levels of the corporate hierarchy. Of the seventy-three Jewish executives in the home offices, approximately two-thirds were found to be in such staff roles as actuaries, physicians, attorneys, or accountants.

Patterns in the Shipping Industry. In addition to its importance as a major employer in this country during the years following World War II, the shipping industry also received large-scale federal government operating and construction subsidies during this time. (At the time of the research studies cited in this section, these industry subsidies amounted to over $300 million a year.) In addition, a second factor that gave this industry symbolic importance was its status as an unofficial representative of the American government to other nations and trading partners.

Within this context, the ADL undertook a study in 1967 to determine the degree of Jewish representation in the industry at the managerial, executive, and director levels. The results of the study were similar to those in the other industries we have examined:

The study of the executive and director levels of the 14 surveyed companies receiving subsidies under the Merchant Marine Acts reveals the almost complete absence from these levels of Jewish personnel. . . . The tabulation shows that of the 14 Federally-subsidized shipping companies, 12 have no Jews whatsoever on their roster of executives and directors. Of the 310 officers and directors listed by the 14 firms, only 3 are Jewish. In percentage terms, this is 9/10 of 1% (*Rights*, 1967, 117–18)

The authors of the report go on to say that two of the firms, when presented with these data, responded positively and expressed concern about their implications. The twelve other companies either did not respond to the information at all or responded in a less than satisfactory manner.

Patterns in the Automobile Industry. For the three decades immediately after World War II, the automobile industry was by far our most dominant industry in terms of its impact on the public psyche, the financial power of the companies, and the number of people employed. One group that was not employed to any extent by the automobile industry during these years was Jews. Despite the fact that during these years in the Detroit area (the traditional main base of the Big Three auto firms of the time), approximately 10 percent of college graduates were Jewish, the industry employed very few Jews at any managerial level. An ADL study in 1963 found that none of the top 128 officers of the Big Three firms was Jewish (Anti-Defamation League, 1963). Consistent with this, it was also found that of the Big Three, Ford employed 146 Jews in white-collar, professional, and technical positions, Chrysler 102, and General Motors 79. This total of 327 was less than 1 percent of the approximately 51,000 such employees in the industry at that time.

Patterns in the Public Utilities. Consistent with the patterns summarized by Belth (1979) in his earlier review, the public utilities continued to employ minimal numbers of Jewish employees at the managerial/executive level during the three decades following World War II. Supporting this conclusion was a *New York Times* article in 1963 that pointed out that approximately 1 percent of all public utility officers nationwide were Jewish (8 of 735) (Spiegal, 1963).

Eight years later, there were few changes, with one notable exception. An American Jewish Committee (1971) study reported that 17 of 942 executives in the public utilities were Jewish, and of these 17, 10 were from one company. This was the Consolidated Edison Company of New York, where a new president, Charles Luce, had implemented such hiring practices to make up for what he felt were previous discriminatory practices. However, Luce was pretty much alone in his attitudes; if we eliminate Consolidated Edison of New York as a special case for this reason, only 7 of the remaining 925 remaining public utility executives in 1971 were Jewish. This is an even lower proportion than was found in 1963.

5
Jews and the Corporate Hierarchy: A Contemporary View

Jay Pritzker of Chicago, a member of one of the richest families in America and reportedly worth from $700 million to $1 billion, obviously has not been hampered by any anti-Semitism there may be in the business community. However, when asked about directorships held by successful Jewish businessmen, he said that he doubted that there are more Jews on boards than in the recent past. "I don't see many Jews on gentile boards, and my guess is there are no more Jews on boards in general than there were ten or twenty years ago, at least not in Chicago."

Simon Rifkind, a corporate lawyer in New York since the 1920's who sat on the boards of Loews and Revlon before he retired, also did not see any change. "The best place to look if you want is in the banking fraternity. Jews have traditionally been successful bankers, and yet if you look at most of the commercial banks you will not find a Jewish name at all, maybe a rarity here and there of late, but almost none. The same is true of the major insurance companies. I would say the same is true of the most of the bigger corporations. I have not made a check to see how many Jews are on the Fortune 500 but I'm very sure that you will find the Jews are members of the boards of firms that have made the 500 which are of Jewish origin or Jewish dominated—not many of the other kind."

Nor did Sidney Brody of Los Angeles, head of his family investment company and a director of the largest bank in the city, think that things had changed on the West Coast. "Not to any great extent," he replied to our question. (Zweigenhaft and Domhoff, 1982, p. 25)

The paradox between Jews' contributions to the American economic enterprise and their lack of presence in managerial/executive roles in corporate America is not just a historical fact of minor relevance to today's world. The discrepancy is as clear today as it has ever been. On the one hand, Jews continue to make major entrepreneurial contributions in the form of new ventures, and they are able to obtain higher-level managerial/executive positions in corporate settings where there has been a history of extensive Jewish family influence, either in the founding of the corporation or in its later development. At the same time, consistent with the outsider hypothesis, Jews continue to be absent from senior management positions in the much larger and much more powerful segments of corporate America from which they have traditionally been absent over the years.

Jewish Presence in the Corporate Elite

The "corporate elite" are generally viewed as those who are at the very top of organizational hierarchies. Although the titles defining such status may vary somewhat from company to company, the elite are typically considered to be the chief executive officers and members of the boards of directors. Since these titles signify individuals who occupy the positions of major and/or final responsibility in decision making, the individuals who fulfill such roles are therefore those who are perceived as having the greatest status or power in the organizations.

Research data on the corporate elite indicate that until about a decade ago, there was a slow but steady growth in the percentage of these individuals who identified themselves as having Jewish backgrounds, *if* we group together all industries and companies. The numbers show that during the first decade of this century, the percentage of Jewish corporate leaders was about 3 percent; it then rose to about 4.5 percent by midcentury and to 7 percent by 1976 (Miller, 1952; Newcomer, 1955; Burck, 1976). However, in line with our earlier discussion of the significance of entrepreneurial opportunities in affecting the manner in which Jews in this country have viewed their career options, Newcomer (1954) pointed out that about 40 percent of the Jewish corporate leaders at midcentury had "organized their own enterprises." Yet, despite this caveat, it may also be that the growth that took place during this period did reflect some real increase in executive opportunities in the general setting of corporate America for Americans of the Jewish faith. This latter, more optimistic view was reinforced in a 1976 article in a *Fortune* magazine study profiling the chief executive officers of 800 major American corporations, of whom approximately 7 percent were estimated to be Jewish (Burck, 1976).

Yet since 1976, this growth, whatever its level, seems to have come to a halt. Since the time of the *Fortune* study, researchers who have focused on this question have found that the percentage of the corporate elite who identify themselves as Jewish has remained stable or perhaps has even declined by a small amount, depending on which study one looks at. In one investigation, Zweigenhaft and Domhoff (quoted in Zweigenhaft, 1984) found that Jews made up between 5 and 7 percent of the corporate directors on *Fortune's* annual list of the largest corporations. Also, a 1986 study of the chief executive officers of the Fortune 500 companies reported that 7.6 percent of the CEOs described themselves as Jewish (McComas, 1986).

Two other studies by Zweigenhaft have reported similar results. In the first of these (Zweigenhaft, 1980), the major focus was on identifying the corporate board memberships of the members of the board of governors of the American Jewish Committee, one of the oldest and most prestigious of the national Jewish organizations and one that has traditionally been oriented toward people who have been successful in the business world. Utilizing board of governors lists for 1952, 1967, 1976, and 1978, Zweigenhaft examined their membership on corporate boards in general and, in particular, their membership on the boards of companies listed in the Fortune 500 and the various Fortune Service 50s (for example, the fifty largest commercial banks, merchandising establishments, transportation companies, insurance companies, and utilities). His results showed that although 33 to 71 percent of these American Jewish Committee board members were also on corporate boards of companies that employed more than 100 people, very few were on the boards of the major companies included in the *Fortune* rankings. In 1967, 6 of the 109 members of the board of governors were also on the board of a Fortune 500 or Fortune 50 company; in 1976, the figures were 9 of 135; and in 1978, 7 of 143. In 1967, no individual was on more than one corporate board. This figure increased to three members on more than one board in 1976 and then fell back to one again in 1978.

In a second study, Zweigenhaft (1982) contrasted the corporate board affiliations of matched samples of 219 Jewish and non-Jewish philanthropists. The results were quite similar to those of his other study. Although the groups were matched, and both groups had large numbers of corporate board affiliations, the findings clearly indicated (as shown in table 5–1) that the Jewish philanthropists were much more likely than the non-Jewish philanthropists to be in smaller companies and much less likely to be in the larger corporations and the centers of corporate power in America.

Considering these patterns, claims for any great degree of progress during the past century, or even during the past decade, appear to be debatable at best. Although there has been a growth in the Jewish percentage of corporate leadership, there is reason to ask

Table 5–1
Relationship between Religious Affiliations of Philanthropists and Corporate Board Memberships

Board Memberships	Jewish Philanthropists (N = 219)	Non-Jewish Philanthropists (N = 219)
Top industrials	1	4
Top 50 industrials	3	14
Top 100 industrials	13	22
Top 200 industrials	24	36
Top 500 industrials	49	53
Top 1,000 industrials	72	61
Top 50 commercial banking companies	8	11
Top 50 diversified financial companies	2	5
Top 50 life insurance companies	3	6
Top 50 retailing companies	11	3
Top 50 transportation companies	4	4
Top 50 utilities	5	4

Source: R. L. Zweigenhaft, "Recent Patterns of Jewish Representation in the Corporate and Social Elites," *Contemporary Jewry* 6(1982), p. 40.

how much of this growth has been due to an opening up of corporate America to actual and potential Jewish executives, as opposed to a continuing pattern in which Jews are essentially limited to ventures and opportunities primarily of their own making. The view of Jews as outsiders in corporate America suggests the latter explanation; that is, there is greater representation of Jews at corporate elite levels in companies with a history of Jewish presence than in companies with no such history. This question is examined later in greater degree.

Also of particular interest in this examination will be the possible reasons for the lack of progress or change during the past decade—supposedly a time in our nation's history of increasing opportunities in corporate America for the so-called outsiders in American life. Before examining such possible explanations, one immediate question that suggests itself is whether such explanations are necessary if one accepts that the 7 percent figure is an asymptote of Jewish presence at the corporate elite level and that such a figure is about as much as one might expect, given that Jews are only 2.5 percent of the American population. Perhaps—yet the same 1986 *Fortune* article that showed that Jews comprise 7.6 percent of our corporate leadership also reported that Episcopalians and Presbyterians, each approximately 2 percent of the American population, nevertheless accounted for approximately 35 percent of the CEO's, in approximately equal proportions. Why should an asymptotic level (if that is what it is) be higher for one religious group than for another? A potentially more useful explanation is suggested by the Ohio State study discussed earlier (tables 3–1 and 3–2), which showed that Episcopalians and Presbyterians are perceived as insiders in American life, while Jews are viewed as outsiders and thus less appropriate for corporate leadership.

Proportions of Jewish Senior Executives: Overall Comparisons across Industries and Companies

Several studies in the research literature provide general, overall estimates of the contemporary Jewish presence at the senior executive

level (that is, those who report to the corporate elite). Although
there is some variation among these surveys, there is a convergence
around a figure of 6 to 8 percent as an overall estimate of the percentage of Jewish senior executives in corporate America. Among
those who have reported overall figures within this range are Sturdivant and Adler (1976), who estimated that 6 percent of a sample
of 444 senior executives were Jewish; Alba and Moore (1982), who
reported a figure of 6.9 percent; and Korn-Ferry International, an
executive search firm, which found in a 1986 survey that 7.4 percent of 4,350 executives of major corporations were Jewish (Bennett, 1986). The Korn-Ferry study is of particular interest for two
reasons. First, the 7.4 percent figure was an increase over the 5.6
percent reported by the same investigators five years earlier. Second, in a more striking exception to the general conclusion, the
Korn-Ferry researchers also reported that Jews accounted for approximately 13 percent of the executives under age forty.

Setting the latter figure aside for a moment, these surveys, taken
in context, suggest a slight increase of perhaps 1 to 2 percent (from
the 6 to 8 percent figure) in the proportion of Jewish senior executives overall during the past decade, with some indication, more
tentatively, that the increase might be continuing. Further support
for this conclusion is provided in an unpublished study conducted
by the American Jewish Committee in Philadelphia, which found a
slight upward trend in the number of Jewish executives among
twenty-three companies in the Philadelphia area over a decade. At
the same time, however, and indicative of the need to go beyond
these overall figures, these same researchers found that there was
continuing evidence of strong resistance to the employment of Jews
at higher levels in a considerable number of organizations in the
Philadelphia area. According to the report:

> In 1984, 15 of the firms studied indicated that Jews in top man-
> agement represented 7.8%. In 1981 the comparable statistic was
> 6.5%. However, the most startling fact is that at present 11 out
> of the 23 or 48% of the companies do not have any Jews in top
> management. Although there has been a slight improvement in
> the past three years in the percentage of Jewish participation . . .

there seems to be a hard core of firms which have resisted and continue to resist promoting or recruiting Jews for top management positions. (Grossman and Stenig, 1985)

Given this rather consistent picture of, at most, an increase of 1 to 2 percent over a decade in the proportion of Jewish senior executives overall, how might we account for the 13 percent figure proposed in 1986 by the Korn-Ferry researchers as an estimate of the percentage of Jewish executives below the age of forty? One possibility is that there really has been a drastic change that has not been picked up in the other studies and that many previously closed corporate opportunities have recently opened up to Jewish managerial aspirants. However, such an explanation would be difficult to integrate with the other data we have reported here or with the recruiting data for a decade ago, which will be examined in a later chapter. It would appear logical that if there were a significant increase in Jewish presence at the senior executive level by the mid-1980s, such individuals would have been recruited in the 1960s and 1970s. The studies to be reviewed suggest no such recruitment activity.

Another possible explanation for the 13 percent figure is that the proportion of Jewish senior executives in a particular company depends on which companies and industries were surveyed. For example, senior executives under the age of forty may be more likely to be found in family-owned firms than in publicly held corporations, a distinction that has already been pointed to as of great significance in understanding the occupational behavior of Jews in this country. Since the selection of Jews for managerial/executive career paths is more likely in a family-owned firm if the family involved is Jewish, it is important that we know the characteristics of the firms surveyed by Korn-Ferry if the 13 percent figure is to be appropriately and accurately interpreted. The more the proportion of family-owned firms in the sample of firms studied, the more likely is that they would find senior executives, including Jewish senior executives, under age forty. Finally, a further reason for having some doubt about the degree to which this 13 percent is an actual indication of the future comes from an article by Rottenberg

(1979). In a general discussion of anti-Semitism in organizational life, he notes that although 15 percent of the student body of the Harvard Graduate School of Business Administration is Jewish, Jews constitute only .5 percent of participants in the Harvard Advanced Management Program, one of the most important training grounds for those being prepared to move into the top levels of corporate management.

Despite these questions and the clear need to go beyond such findings, studies of the overall level of Jewish presence at the senior executive level in American industry are important and useful on several grounds. The figures, in and of themselves, are of value because they suggest overall trends in the proportion of Jewish senior executives, and a knowledge of overall trends is important for certain policy issues and theoretical questions of a macrosocietal nature. One of the more important values is that these studies suggest useful diagnostic guidelines that enable us to classify industries according to their relative level of Jewish presence at the managerial and/or executive levels—that is, higher or lower than the average. The figure of 6 to 8 percent enables us to identify and classify those industries in which opportunities for employment of Jews who are interested in managerial/executive career paths might be considered to be pretty much at the norm level for corporate America, as opposed to those in which such opportunities are less or more likely to be available—that is, above or below the norm. A second benefit of such guidelines or norms is that they also enable us to ascertain how industries with different proportions of Jewish executives and potential employment opportunities for future Jewish managerial career aspirants differ from one another in terms of size, financial opportunities, growth possibilities, potential or actual societal significance, and so forth. These normative guidelines thus give us a clearer overall understanding of (1) variations in corporate America in their degree of openness to employment of Jews along managerial/executive career paths, (2) the industries and companies in which changes might have taken place over time, and (3) those employers whose view of Jews as outsiders appears to be continuing to operate as a negative influence on their potential for managerial/executive career opportunities.

Jewish Presence in the Corporate Hierarchy:
Industry Variations

Studies of the proportion of Jewish senior executives in various major industries indicate several characteristics and patterns for such employment. One pattern is that there is a minimal level of Jewish presence at the executive level in major American industries that employ millions of people and account for billions of dollars in sales. These studies also show that those industries in which the Jewish presence is now minimal are generally the same industries in which a Jewish presence has been minimal in the past and—consistent with the view of Jews as outsiders in American life—in which there is no history of a Jewish family influence. Thus, even in those industries in which there are companies that do employ significant numbers of Jews at the executive levels, there are also companies in which the level of Jewish presence is minimal.

Examination of the research findings shows that these differences are related to the history of the companies, thus supporting the outsider hypothesis. There are Jewish executives at the senior management levels if there has been or is a Jewish family influence in a company, but if there has been no such influence, the likelihood of significant numbers of Jewish senior executives is much less. In addition, both in industries in which there are generally few Jews and in industries in which companies vary in their degree of employment of Jewish executives, there are strong relationships suggesting that the larger the company, the less likely it is to employ Jews at the managerial/executive level. The success of Jewish Americans as entrepreneurs and as developers and managers of corporations making significant contributions to the American economy seems to have had little impact on the selection and promotion patterns of major segments of corporate America. Over the years, there has been little apparent change among these industries and companies in the degree to which they have avoided recruiting, selecting, and developing Jewish Americans for managerial/executive career paths.

The following section describes in detail the methods and findings of a research investigation I conducted that has provided major evidence for these conclusions.

Industry and Company Variations
in Jewish Presence at Senior Management Levels

The purpose of the study to be described in this section was to ascertain the percentage of executives in contemporary corporate America who could be identified as Jewish and to determine how such percentages varied for industries and organizations that differ from one another in annual sales and number of employees. Of particular interest in the research was determining the percentage of Jewish executives and the degree of such variation in the types of industries and companies represented in both the Fortune 500 and the Fortune Service 500. In general, the research was governed by the following overall questions:

1. In what industries and companies does one find higher and/ or lower levels of Jewish presence at the executive levels?

2. In what ways do industries and companies that differ from one another in terms of the percentage of Jewish senior executives also differ from one another in terms of such measures as annual sales and number of employees?

Methods

The procedure utilized for assessing the number of Jewish executives in each firm was to classify those names that were clearly Jewish-sounding and those that were not from the listings of senior executives and corporate officers provided for each company in *The Corporate 1000* (1985), a compendium that lists such employees for the top 1,000 American corporations. In cases of doubt, the classification decision was resolved by using as guidelines the names listed by Slavin and Pradt (1982) and the names listed in various telephone directories of Jewish organizations and publications.

Since there are clearly questions that may be raised by the use of such a procedure, some discussion of the validity and reliability of the method would seem to be in order before we proceed. One problem stems from the fact that there are obviously some Jews who have non-Jewish names and some non-Jews who have Jewish names. Both these errors in classification are possible, and both have undoubtedly entered in here to an unknown extent. Yet there are countervailing considerations that should be kept in mind. One such consideration is that most Jews in this country have Jewish-sounding names and most non-Jews do not. Thus, there is a built-in base rate of accuracy in this method that has to be considered against possible misclassifications to determine an overall accuracy rate. (For example, if thirty-five individuals with very Jewish-sounding names are classified as Jewish and one who is Jewish is not classified as such because he has a non-Jewish-sounding name—such as Smith—the rate of error in the method is one out of thirty-six, or less than 3 percent.)

A second factor to consider is that classification errors in this procedure may be made in both directions. For example, there may be Smiths who would not be classified as Jewish by this method but who may, in fact, be Jewish, and there may also be individuals with such names as Lehman and Cohen who would be counted as Jewish but who might not be. (In 1985, the secretary of the navy was named Lehman, and an assistant chaplain at Yale and a U.S. Senator from Maine were both named Cohen. None of these individuals happens to be Jewish.)

Another potential source of error with this method may not be an error at all from a conceptual perspective. I refer here to those Jews who changed their names in order to avoid the appearance of being Jewish—an avoidance they obviously believed was necessary if they were to have a chance at corporate success as a manager. Is it an error to count these individuals as non-Jewish, as we did by utilizing this method? It may not be, given our major concern with the implications of being Jewish for managerial success in the corporate world. Such individuals, by their act of name-changing, give clear behavioral testimony to the perceived existence of such difficulties. Perhaps they should not be counted as Jewish, since from the corporate viewpoint and their own, they are not.

One recent illustration of this latter point is the case of Harry Gray, the dominant figure in United Technologies Corporation—one of the major industrial corporations in the United States, ranking in the top twenty of the Fortune 500 listings, with over $16 billion a year in sales and more than 200,000 employees. Among its major divisions are Pratt and Whitney, one of our largest suppliers of jet engines for both commercial and military aircraft; Sikorsky helicopters; Carrier air conditioners; and Otis elevators. Despite considerable controversy, Mr. Gray has had major responsibility for the growth of the company to its current high position. He is, by all measures, a prominent figure in corporate America.

There is also considerable evidence that Mr. Gray, despite his denials, was born and raised Jewish and lived as a Jew until he was past thirty, when he changed his name, his life, and apparently his background (Harr, 1985). According to the accounts of relatives and other records, Harry Gray is actually Harry Jack Grusin, the son of Jacob Grusin, a Jewish immigrant from Latvia. According to these accounts, Harry Grusin was raised in a Jewish family, was married under this name in 1946 in a Jewish ceremony to Miss Ina Ruth Palman of Chicago, but left her and a daughter she had borne in 1948, eventually changing his name legally to Harry Jack Gray at the age of thirty-one.

Gray today denies that his name change had anything to do with his Jewishness and, in fact, denies that he is Jewish, a denial that is disputed by his relatives. Gray claims that he was raised as a Presbyterian, and he shows a baptismal certificate as evidence for his claim. However, the baptismal certificate, dated 1982, refers to an event that supposedly took place fifty-three years earlier and for which only one witness could be found, a woman who was twelve years old at the time. Less in dispute is the fact that Gray does not list his parents' names in the biography submitted to *Who's Who*, nor does he list the daughter from his first marriage. Also, in his 1979 marriage application, there is no mention of his first marriage, and his father's name is listed as John Gray, rather than Jacob Grusin.

Regardless of the facts in the Gray case, it is clear that Mr. Gray, whatever his background, does not consider himself Jewish, nor does he wish the world of corporate America to so consider him. From the viewpoint of the research we will be reporting here, he was, most appropriately, not considered Jewish.

It would appear, then, that these considerations provide conceptual justifications for the use of names as a guide to the classification of individuals as Jewish or non-Jewish. There is also empirical support for the validity of this method in a study by Ritterband and Cohen (1984). In an extensive comparative study of the utility of the names method for identifying American Jews, as compared to more complex procedures, they found very similar results between a simple method of identifying Jews on the basis of name identifications from telephone directories and the more complex, expensive technique known as modified random-digit telephone dialing. In one comparison, they found great similarity between the two procedures in terms of demographic characteristics, socioeconomic status, Jewishness, and service usage. Similarly, when they compared their results with those of local newspaper studies that had used complex random-digit dialing procedures exclusively, the proportion of Jewish households estimated for the boroughs of New York with the two techniques were virtually identical (18.8 percent versus 18.3 percent).

Finally, two other checks of the names method also suggest a high degree of comparability of this technique to other approaches. One check compared the median figure for the proportion of Jewish executives in all industries obtained by this method with the figures obtained by methods used in other studies. The overall figure obtained by this method, 6.2 percent, was slightly higher than the 5.6 percent figure cited by Sturdivant and Adler (1976) but slightly lower than the 6.9 percent figure in the Alba and Moore (1982) study and the 7.4 percent figure cited by Korn-Ferry (Bennett, 1986). In a further check on the validity of the names method, the proportion of Jewish representatives in a randomly chosen sample of thirty-eight corporate boards of directors was compared to the figures reported by Zweigenhaft and Domhoff (1982). The results were identical—6 percent—in each case.

One further estimate of the value of the method concerned the test–retest reliability of the classifications obtained. Three separate samples—classified one week, two weeks, and one month apart—generated reliabilities in all cases of over 90 percent, a figure highly acceptable for social science research purposes.

Having checked the validity and reliability of the names method and its comparability to the techniques used by others, Jewish presence at the senior executive level in different industries was then estimated by grouping the figures obtained for companies into industries based on the classifications utilized by *Fortune* magazine in its study of American corporations (Sellars, 1985). In the following discussion of industry variations, it is these groupings that will serve as the basis for our analyses.

Findings

The Fortune 500: Industry Comparisons. Overall, the results indicated that the industries comprising the Fortune 500 could be classified into three groups, according to the proportion of senior executives who were Jewish. Group A consisted of those industries in which the proportion of Jewish executives was estimated to be below 5 percent. This figure corresponds roughly to 1 percent below the lowest level of the estimates made on the basis of surveys of the proportion of Jewish executives in American industry overall—that is, 6 to 8 percent. The decision to use 5 percent, rather than 6 percent, as the cutoff for Group A was based on the desirability of a further correction of possible misclassifications by the names method and an attempt to be as conservative as possible about categorizing industries and/or companies as "low" in the proportion of senior executives who are Jewish. Under this same rationale, Group B consisted of those industries that were estimated to have Jewish presence at the senior executive level at about the norm for corporate America—that is, from 5 to 8 percent—and Group C consisted of those industries in which the proportion of Jewish executives was found to be above the norm for American corporations, or greater than 8 percent.

Group A: Industries with Low Proportions of Jewish Senior Executives (Less than 5 Percent). Table 5–2 lists the industries in Group A, their estimated percentages of Jewish senior executives, the total sales of each industry in 1984, and the number of employees in each industry. To increase comparability, the figures for each industry in table 5–2 are based on the nine largest companies in the industry for which complete data could be obtained from both *Fortune* and the *Washington Monitor*.

Table 5–2

Industries with Low Proportions of Jewish Senior Executives

Industry	Percentage Jewish Senior Executives	Industry Sales ($billions)	Number of Employees (000)
Petroleum	0.7	336	757
Chemicals	2.3	90	637
Food	3.3	61	499
Glass, building materials	3.5	20	197
Mining, crude oil production	3.9	48	128
Pharmaceuticals	4.0	35	368
Precision instruments	4.3	36	435
Rubber and plastic	4.3	27	334
Beverages	4.3	28	279
Motor vehicles and parts	4.4	180	1,446
Metal manufacturing	4.5	38	283
Totals		899	5,363

The most defining characteristic of Group A is that it includes many of the largest, most powerful industries in corporate America, accounting for almost $900 billion a year in sales and employing more than 5 million people. Although most industries represented are the traditional "hard" industries, this is not totally the case; there is actually considerable diversity in Group A—for example, foods, pharmaceuticals, precision instruments, and beverages. It may also be noted that in some of these industries, there is a lack of Jewish executives even though the particular industries may have been marked by major contributions from Jewish entrepreneurs in the past. In a point we will return to later, although the data indicate that a Jewish family background in a company has made it more likely that there will be Jewish senior executives, the presence of such a background, either now or in the past, has not constituted an ironclad guarantee that increased employment and career opportunities have existed for Jewish would-be executives.

Two more industries that also belong to Group A had to be analyzed separately because of an insufficient number of companies. These industries are shipbuilding/railroad/transportation and tobacco. In the former case, data from six companies were used to estimate a 4.9 percent proportion of Jewish executives for a group of companies that accounted for $9 billion annually in sales and

employed approximately 121,000 employees. The comparable estimates for the tobacco industry, based on four companies, were a 4
percent proportion of Jewish executives, $27 billion in sales, and
251,000 employees. If we add the figures for these industries to
those presented in table 5–2, we can then estimate that Group A—
the group below the norm in the employment of Jewish executives—accounts, in total, for approximately $935 billion a year in
sales and employs approximately 5,635,000 individuals.

*Group B: Industries with Percentages of Jewish Executives at
the Nationwide Norm (5.0 to 7.9 percent).* Table 5–3 lists industries in which the proportion of Jewish senior executives was found
to be approximately within the range identified in previous surveys
as descriptive for American corporations overall.

The results shown in table 5–3 differ significantly from those
in table 5–2 in several ways. One difference is that far fewer industries are shown in table 5–3. As a result, Group B represents a far
smaller segment of corporate America in terms of both annual sales
and number of employees. Compared to the industries comprising
Group A, the industries in Group B have slightly more than one-
third the total dollar sales and approximately two-thirds the employee population. A second difference is that the companies in
Group B are, on the average, smaller in annual sales than the com-

Table 5–3

*Industries with Percentages of Jewish Senior Executives Level
at the Nationwide Norm*

Industry	Percentage Jewish Senior Executives	Industry Sales ($billions)	Number of Employees (000)
Electronics, appliances	5.0	112	1156
Office equipment, computers	5.1	84	938
Forest products	5.2	38	255
Metal products	5.6	14	146
Industrial, farm equipment	6.5	27	305
Aerospace	7.8	74	805
Soaps, cosmetics	7.9	29	182
Totals		378	3787

panies in Group A. If we compute the average annual sales for each company in Group A ($N = 109$) and Group B ($N = 63$), the average company in Group A accounts for approximately $8.5 billion annually in sales, whereas the comparable figure in Group B is $6 billion. However, the average size of the employee work force of the Group B companies is somewhat larger (60,000) than the average figure for the Group A organizations (51,600).

Group C: Industries with Above-Norm Percentages of Jewish Senior Executives (8.0 percent or Greater). Table 5–4 lists industries in which the proportion of Jewish senior executives was found to be higher than the normative level found in overall surveys.

There were only three industries for which nine companies could clearly be identified that had a higher than average proportion of Jewish senior executives. A fourth industry, which was also categorized into Group C but for which only three companies could be clearly classified, was the toy industry. In this case, the relevant figures were 25 percent Jewish senior executives, $2 billion a year in sales and 33,000 employees. Including the toy industry, the total figures for Group C were approximately $47 billion a year in sales and 649,000 employees. These figures are approximately 5 percent and 12 percent, respectively, of Group A and 12 percent and 17 percent, respectively, of Group B. In addition to these figures showing the minimal significance of the Group C companies relative to those in Groups A and B, the firms in Group C were also found to be far smaller in terms of both average annual dollar sales and average employee population. The average dollar volume per company

Table 5–4

Industries with Above-Norm Percentages
of Jewish Senior Executives

Industry	Percentage Jewish Senior Executives	Industry Sales ($billions)	Number of Employees (000)
Publishing, printing	9.5	18	180
Textiles, vinyl flooring	9.9	12	184
Apparel	26.7	15	252
Totals		45	616

in Group C ($N = 3$) is $1.6 billion (as compared to $8.5 billion
for Group A and $6 billion for Group B), and the average number
of employees is approximately 21,600 (as compared to 51,600 for
Group A and 60,000 for Group B).

Differences among Companies. Comparisons among industries are
useful, but they do not answer a number of significant questions.
Examining the characteristics of a particular industry as a unit does
not take into account the possibility of significant variation among
the companies that make up that industry. For industries in which
the overall proportion of Jewish executives is very low—such as
those in Group A—this point is probably moot, for very little intercompany variation is possible when the overall level for an industry
is no more than 3 percent. However, the point is more relevant in
industries in which there is a higher level of Jewish representation—
such as the industries in Groups B and C. An important question
for the latter groups is whether there is a generally similar proportion of Jewish senior executives in companies throughout a particular industry, as opposed to significant intercompany variation. The
question is important on several counts. One reason is that the answer provides us with some understanding of how the occupational
opportunity system has worked in a particular segment of corporate
America. From a conceptual perspective, one may argue that if the
proportion of Jewish executives is fairly similar among companies
in an industry, then a key factor in determining the proportion of
Jewish executives in the organizations involved may be the characteristics of that industry. Some industries, perhaps because of certain structural characteristics, may lend themselves more to an acceptance of a Jewish presence than others. Perhaps the fact of a
lower level of required original capital investment and the general
openness to entrepreneurial ventures by Jews (and others) that this
generated led, in turn, to a more general "openness," which became
part of these industries. Alternatively, we may find an asymmetry
in a particular industry that has a significant proportion of Jewish
executives; some of the companies may have more Jewish manag-
ers/executives than the norm and other companies in the same industry may have fewer. If such asymmetry is found, a different sce-
nario   would   have   to   be   developed,   both   for   conceptual

understanding and for developing guidelines for occupational choice for aspirants, Jewish and non-Jewish, to managerial roles in that industry. If asymmetry is found in a particular industry, we might feel justified in concluding that the openness of that industry in providing executive career opportunities for Jews may have less to do with such factors as the capital investment or other structural characteristics of that industry and more to do with the people involved in a particular company. It is this question of the degree and nature of the degree of variation among companies in an industry that concerns us in this analysis.

Table 5–5 summarizes differences among the companies within the industries classified into Groups B and C. The data indicate that there is considerable variation in the proportions of Jewish executives among the companies within each industry, thus supporting the asymmetry view.

Table 5–5

Within-Industry Company Differences in Numbers of Jewish Senior Executives

Industries	Companies with Two or More Jewish Senior Executives			Companies with Fewer Than Two Jewish Senior Executives		
	No. of Companies	Annual Sales ($billions)	No. of Employees (000)	No. of Companies	Annual Sales ($billions)	No. of Employees (000)
Aerospace	4	37	435	5	38	370
Electronics	4	50	604	5	62	552
Industrial and farm equipment	3	8	141	6	20	164
Metal products	2	5	57	7	9	87
Office equipment and computers	3	13	184	6	71	754
Forest Products	3	11	95	6	28	160
Soaps, cosmetics	7	24	139	2	5	43
Textiles/vinyl/floors	3	4	71	6	7	113
Publishing, printing	5	12	84	4	8	96
Apparel	6	13	196	3	2	56
Totals	40	177	2006	50	250	2647

In both Groups B and C, there are some companies in each
industry with a minimal number of Jewish senior executives (no
more than one) and others with two or more. The conclusion is as
true for those companies in Group C as for those in Group B. Even
in industries such as apparel, publishing/printing, and textiles/
vinyl/floors—all of which have companies with significant numbers of Jewish executives—there are also companies with few Jewish executives and which are indistinguishable, at least in terms of
this characteristic, from the overwhelming number of firms that
comprise the industries in Group A.

These patterns suggest that the factors that generate a significant Jewish presence in an industry once the industry develops are
not so much a function of the structural characteristics of that industry as a function of the individuals within a particular company
who make the employment decisions. The levels of capital investment required by an industry may influence the possibility and ease
of entrepreneurial ventures, thus enabling entrance into that industry, regardless of personal characteristics, so long as individuals
stay within the firms in which they begin. This is one of the most
admirable and most desirable characteristics of a free marketplace.
At the same time, however, we apparently have to distinguish between ease of entry in an economic sense and the operation of other
factors regarding employment possibilities. Table 5–5 suggests that
the view of Jews as outsiders in corporate America has apparently
operated as an impediment to employment at the executive level in
some corporate settings even in industries in which Jews have made
significant entrepreneurial and managerial contributions. In each of
the industries listed in table 5–5, including industries with companies that have had significant previous levels of Jewish entrepreneurial contribution, there are some companies in which the level of
Jewish employment is minimal or virtually nonexistent and there
are some companies in which it is higher than the norm. Such dis-
parities are systematic and consistent across industries, and they are
in keeping with the evidence presented earlier.

An Analysis of the Fortune 100. The Fortune 100 companies are
frequently viewed as the elite corporations of America. Regardless
of the industry in which a particular corporation operates, the com-

panies comprising the Fortune 100 are those that make the headlines and serve as the subjects of frequent legal, media, and scholarly examination. They are the pacesetters of corporate America in marketing, strategic planning, human resource management, and the design of production systems. In brief, the companies that comprise the Fortune 100 are those that most often come to mind when we think of the organizations that symbolize American industry.

Table 5–6 lists the percentage of Jewish executives at the senior management level in companies comprising the Fortune 100. As guidelines for our breakdowns, we have used the same percentages used previously in defining Groups A, B, and C. In addition, table 5–6 also provides the annual dollar sales of each group and the number of employees.

Of the hundred companies listed in the Fortune 100, seventy-three may be categorized as low (Group A) in terms of the propor-

Table 5–6

Percentages of Jewish Senior Executives in Fortune 100 Companies

Fortune Group	No. of Companies with this Percentage of Jewish Executives		
	<5%	5–8%	>8%
1–20	15	1	4
Annual sales ($billions)	589	61	36
No. of employees (000)	2,341	570	130
21–40	15	4	1
Annual sales ($billions)	99	28	11
No. of employees (000)	1,563	246	115
41–60	14	2	4
Annual sales ($billions)	109	7	22
No. of employees (000)	908	91	182
61–80	12	2	6
Annual sales ($billions)	71	15	21
No. of employees (000)	636	182	303
81–100	17	0	3
Annual sales ($billions)	66	4	12
No. of employees (000)	784	45	113
Totals	73	9	18
Annual sales ($billions)	934	115	102
No. of employees (000)	6,232	1,134	843

tion of Jewish senior executives according to the criteria we have
defined, nine belong in Group B, and eighteen are in Group C.
The practical significance of such differences in terms of potential
employment opportunities is reflected in the disparity between these
groups in terms of annual dollar sales and number of employees.
The firms that employ few Jews at the senior management level
(Group A) have over four times the annual sales level of the other
two groups combined and over three times the number of employees.

The results of this analysis of the Fortune 100 are consistent
with our industry analyses on two levels. Nearly three-quarters of
these major American corporations are below the nationwide norm
in terms of the proportion of Jewish senior executives employed.
Also, even within the restricted range of companies implied by this
type of analysis, the Jewish absence from corporate America is
greatest in the larger companies, as it was in the larger industries.
The more a company can be characterized by high sales levels and
a large number of employees, the more likely it is that that company
will be unlikely to have Jewish senior executives.

The Fortune Service 500: Comparisons among Industries and Com-
panies. The Fortune 500 rankings include only firms and industries
in the manufacturing/production segment of the American economy. Although the distinction between production and service
functions is sometimes difficult to make because of the complexity
of many of the organizations involved, the Fortune 500 normally
does not include firms and industries whose major focus is provi-
sion of services of some kind. *Fortune* does rank these service companies in terms of sales levels and employee population, but it first
differentiates them into groups according to the types of services
provided. These separate group rankings are then sometimes reclas-
sified in their entirety as the Fortune Service 500. Since any attempt
to assess the proportion of Jewish senior executives in the American
work setting must include representation from the service area of
the economy as well as the manufacturing area, research analyses
comparable to those undertaken for the Fortune 500 were also undertaken for the Fortune Service 500.

Table 5–7 presents the basic data on the percentages of Jewish Americans at the senior executive level for eight of these service industries. There are two groups of industries in table 5–7. One group has a low proportion of Jewish senior executives and is therefore comparable to the industries classified as Group A in the analysis of the Fortune 500. The other group has a higher than average proportion of Jewish executives and is therefore comparable to Group C.

The four industries in the low category (less than 5 percent) present few surprises; each appeared earlier in our discussion as industries in which there has been minimal Jewish presence in the past. Table 5–7 indicates that there has been little change from the patterns noted in earlier years. Such lack of change is important in itself. Just as important are the size and significance of the "low" industries listed in table 5–7:

Table 5–7
*Percentages of Jewish Senior Executives
in Service-Related Industries*

Industry	Percentage Jewish Executives
Utilities (8)[a]	1.9
Transportation (9)	2.3
Commercial banking (10)	3.4
Life insurance (9)	4.9
Diversified services (10)[b]	9.3
Diversified financial (10)[b]	9.7
Retailing chains (10)[c]	20.9
Supermarket chains (10)[c]	21.2

[a]Numbers in parentheses are the number of companies included in the analysis for each industry.

[b]The distinction between the diversified services and diversified financial industries is not always clear. Basically, the former group provides services relating to particular products and goods, and the latter group deals primarily with services relating to money.

[c]Although retailing chains and supermarket chains are combined in the 1985 Fortune Service 500 rankings, they have been separated here because of the different kinds of marketing efforts involved.

1. The commercial banks included in this group have more than $700 billion in assets and employ between 3.5 million and 4 million people.

2. The transportation companies have well over $50 billion a year in operating revenues and employ more than 400,000 people.

3. The utility companies have more than $180 billion in assets and employ between 650,000 and 700,000 people.

4. The life insurance companies have more than $370 billion in assets and employ more than 180,000 people.

The utilities, commercial banking, and life insurance industries alone have well over $1 trillion in assets and employ more than 4 million people. They are major centers of American economic strength and employment and comprise a significant segment of corporate America. However, the presence of Jewish Americans in these industries has been minimal in the past and remains minimal today. Of particular interest in illustrating these conclusions is the case of commercial banking.

A Case Study: Jewish Americans and Commercial Banking. The commercial banking industry is relevant to the concerns of this book for several reasons. One consideration is the discrepancy between historically based prejudice against members of the Jewish faith on the basis of their so-called ties to the banking industry and the historical realities in the United States—that Jews have traditionally been kept out of any major role in the commercial banking industry. A second consideration is that the traditionally low number of Jewish executives at senior levels in the commercial banking industry has occurred despite the fact that many of the most significant career opportunities in this field have been in areas of the country where there are significant numbers of Jewish residents (for example, New York, Chicago, Los Angeles, Washington). Whereas the percentage of college graduates (the usual labor market for managerial/executive hiring) who are Jewish is approximately 10 percent nationwide (Cohen, 1983), the figure is considerably higher in the cities where the centers of commercial banking are located. A third reason for our particular interest in commercial banking is that the absence of Jewish senior executives has become even more noticeable in recent years in contrast to the situation in investment banking, in which some of the most important firms have provided increasing numbers of significant career opportunities to Jewish aspirants.

In general, the characteristics of commercial banking in the past are still the case today. Most of the available evidence indicates that our major commercial banks have not recruited actively where there might be Jewish applicants and continue not to do so (see chapter 6). Similarly, few Jews are appointed to higher-level positions. The figures shown in table 5–7 are little different from the figures that were collected for this same industry a decade ago and that have been collected in other settings. Regardless of the investigator and the method, however, the results have been consistent. In an unpublished report dated February 1976, which is summarized in table 5–8, the Anti-Defamation League (ADL) of B'nai

Table 5–8

*Percentages of Jews in Commercial Banking Top Management,
According to Geographic Area*

Area	N	Percentage Jewish Executives	Percentage of Jews in Geographic Area
Nationwide	1,869	3.37	
Nationwide[a]	1,758[a]	2.56	
New York	406[a]	6.45	25
New York[a]	295[a]	2.70	25
Los Angeles	74	4.04	15
San Francisco	121	4.96	10
Chicago	110	2.73	7
Detroit	97	4.12	5
Philadelphia	98	4.85	17

Source: Anti-Defamation League of B'rai B'rith, "Jewish Presence in Major U.S. Commercial Banking," Unpublished preliminary report, February 1976.

[a]Two separate figures are presented for the nationwide totals and for the New York metropolitan area because eighteen of the sixty-three Jewish top management executives nationwide and twenty-six in the New York area are associated with one New York bank. The influence of this unusual pattern is indicated by showing the figures for the country and for New York first including and then excluding that one bank.

B'rith found a consistent nationwide pattern: The percentages of Jews in top management for fifty leading commercial banks in different geographic areas were far below the percentages of Jews in those areas.

The ADL findings concerning the New York area have been supported in other studies. In a survey by Slavin and Pradt (1982) of some of the personnel practices of New York metropolitan area commercial banks during a time when approximately *one-half* of the college graduates in the New York metropolitan area were Jewish, it was found that *none* of the top executive officers of the top seven commercial banks at the time were Jewish. The comparable figures for the senior managers were 3 of 86 (about 4 percent of the total) and for the senior officers about 16 of 345 (also about 4 percent of the total).

More recently, the American Jewish Committee (AJC) of Philadelphia, as part of the continuing research project cited earlier, undertook a separate analysis of higher-level management of the seven commercial banks included in the twenty-three firms being monitored regularly. The results suggested that there has been little progress during the past decade. In 1972, 4 of 111 top managers were Jewish (3.6 percent); in 1976, 7 of 106 (6.6 percent); in 1981, 7 of 151 (4.6 percent); and in 1984, 8 of 140 (5.7 percent). The report also pointed out that three of the seven banks had no Jewish executives at all in top corporate management and that in 1984 there were actually fewer Jews (two) at the second level of corporate management in the Philadelphia commercial banking industry than there were at the top level (six). This latter finding, it may be noted, provides negative evidence for any time-lag hypothesis that the situation is improving and that it is just a matter of time before a Jewish presence in commercial banking begins to manifest itself. The longitudinal monitoring research being carried out by the AJC in Philadelphia suggests that the "time-lag" explanation for the scarcity of Jewish senior executives in commercial banking top management is not very viable, at least at present.

Service Industries with a Significant Jewish Presence: Intercompany Comparisons. The four industries in table 5–7 that have a significant Jewish presence (diversified services, diversified financial, retailing chains, and supermarket chains) exhibit patterns similar to those we have noted for Groups B and C in the Fortune 500. Each of the four industries includes major firms that have a significant Jewish presence and also companies in which the proportion of Jewish executives is minimal and is not significantly different from most of the firms in industries classified as having few Jewish executives overall (that is, Group A). More specifically:

1. Of the ten largest firms listed in the diversified financial industry, the percentage of Jewish executives in four firms is 8 percent or better. However, the percentage in one firm is less than 1 percent, while the others range from about 2 percent to 7 percent.

2. Of the ten largest firms listed in the diversified services industry, the percentage of Jewish executives in three of these companies ranges from better than 10 percent to nearly 50 percent. However, in five firms listed in this group, the percentage of Jews is less than 1 percent, while the figure for the other two companies is between 2 percent and 5 percent.

3. There are two distinct groups among the fourteen largest general retailing firms (including department store chains). One group of seven companies accounts for $86 billion in sales annually and employs slightly more than 1.1 million people. The percentage of Jewish senior executives (summing over all firms in this group of companies) is approximately 3.3 percent, a figure that puts this industry clearly into the Group A category—industries with a minimal Jewish presence. The second group of companies, also consisting of seven firms with types of businesses very similar to those in the first group, is different in three ways. One difference is that they are not as big, accounting for approximately $54 billion in sales annually and employing approximately 750,000 people. The second difference is that the percentage of Jewish executives in these firms is approximately 25 percent. Third—supporting the outsider hypothesis—virtually all of the companies in the second group of retailing companies, with one exception, have Jewish family backgrounds.

4. There are also two distinct groups in the supermarket industry. In the eight largest supermarket firms in the country, accounting for approximately $76 billion a year in annual sales and em-

ploying approximately 750,000 people, approximately 3.2 percent of the senior executives were Jewish. In contrast to this is a second group of companies, chosen because they were the largest listed for which Jewish family backgrounds could be identified. This group, which consisted of three companies accounting for approximately $10 billion a year in annual sales and employing approximately 125,000 people, had a percentage of Jewish executives of approximately 50 percent. The conclusion is the same here as for general retailing; each industry contains firms with a significant Jewish presence and firms without a significant Jewish presence. However, there are more firms without a significant Jewish presence, the firms are larger, and—supporting the outsider hypothesis—they are less likely to have Jewish family backgrounds.

How Do Jews Become Chief Executive Officers and Members of the Board? Further Evidence for the Importance of the Insider-Outsider Factor in Executive Selection

Considering the data presented in this chapter and the support they provide for the outsider hypothesis, how do Jewish Americans become chief executive officers (CEOs) of corporations that have not been their own ventures or that are not part of a family heritage? On occasion, Jews have become chief executive officers or board members of such companies. How has this taken place?

Empirical research studies, such as that by Zweigenhaft and Domhoff (1982), and historical case study analyses relevant to this question support the outsider hypothesis further. Such analyses show that when Jews become chief executive officers and members of the boards of directors through nonentrepreneurial, nonfamilial routes, it is generally in ways that reflect their outsider status rather than through the vertical mobility we associate with corporate careers and acceptance as "one of the group." A research study by Zweigenhaft and Domhoff (1982) on the patterns by which Jews attain CEO positions in American corporations (in which they do not have ownership) and/or membership on the boards of directors found that in the few cases where this has happened, Jewish CEOs and board members have followed paths that reflect an outsider status. Examination of such paths suggests that upwardly mobile Jewish managers may face considerable difficulty if they attempt to attain corporate success by following the "typical" corporate lifestyle.

The alternative "outsider" paths to board membership and the CEO position may be of several types. Sometimes the board members or CEOs have been lawyers, sometimes investment bankers, and sometimes academics. One famous example is Irving Shapiro, an attorney who came to the attention of DuPont while he was working with the Justice Department and who then moved into the DuPont legal framework, eventually becoming CEO during the mid-1970s and then serving admirably for most of the decade following. Other examples of this pattern have been Simon Rifkind, a Jewish lawyer who came from the "outside" to serve on a number of corporate boards, and, from the field of investment banking, Sidney Weinberg. Weinberg served on many corporate boards during his career, including that of the Ford Motor Company—after the company had been taken over by the grandson of Henry Ford, the publisher of the violently anti-Semitic *Dearborn Independent* a generation earlier.

> The most traditional way to the top for non-Jews—a slow 20–30 year climb up the corporate ladder of a company not founded or purchased by Jews—is the least accessible route for Jewish aspirants. Despite Irving Shapiro's optimism that his appointment to head DuPont signalled the dropping of barriers, Zweigenhaft and Domhoff found no other chief Jewish executive officers who had worked their way up through non-Jewish companies and few Jewish inside directors of such companies. (Zweigenhaft, 1984, p. 8)

Consistent with the perception of Jews as outsiders in much of corporate America, Zweigenhaft (1984) reports that the patterns are normally different in companies with a "Jewish history"—that is, companies that were founded by Jews, where the influence of a Jewish family remains strong, and where the company leadership has remained active in the Jewish community. For example, at the time of the Zweigenhaft and Domhoff study, there were at least two Jews on the boards of such companies as CBS, General Dynamics, Levi Strauss, Seagrams, Stop and Shop, and Witco Chemicals. All of these companies were either founded by Jews or were under the control and influence of a Jewish family for a long period in their development—a pattern that generally means that the "outsider" problem is a less significant factor influencing personnel decision making at the executive level.

It is important to note, however, that being in a company with a Jewish history is not invariably positive for Jews who aspire to executive careers. The case of Edward Gudeman, a Jewish executive for thirty-two years at Sears Roebuck, the largest department store chain in this country and now increasingly strong in the financial services field, is particularly illustrative of this paradox. Gudeman was highly regarded as a merchandising innovator and at one point was viewed as a logical choice to eventually succeed to the head position at Sears. However, he was unfortunate enough to be at Sears during the time when Robert Wood was chairman. Wood was an open anti-Semite who made it clear that he would never allow a Jew to become president of Sears even though the largest stockholders in Sears at the time were the Rosenwalds, a prominent Jewish family, and even though Wood, himself, had succeeded a Rosenwald. As a result Gudeman was passed over in favor of another individual more acceptable to Wood; a person who, in the opinion of many, was nowhere near the level of Gudeman and whose appointment led to the departure of a number of executives at Sears, including that of Gudeman himself. Furthermore, even though these events were, in the view of some financial analysts, responsible at least in part for Sears' problems during the 1960s and 1970s, the fact was that the situation at Sears remained the same even into the 1970s when only one of thirty-nine corporate officers was Jewish and the managerial level immediately below was also relatively bereft of Jews (Rottenberg, 1979).

The Sears history is not unique. Similar attitudes regarding the selection of Jewish Americans for higher-level positions have been noted in several other major American corporations owned and/or under the control of Jewish families. For years, the Newhouse family, owners of a large newspaper and magazine publishing empire, has reputedly had a policy of hiring only non-Jews as editors of its publications (except when family members were available) (Krefetz, 1982). Although this no longer seems to be the case, such a pattern also reputedly existed at the *New York Times* during the era when the individuals managing that famous institution were Adolph Ochs and Arthur Hays Sulzberger, both Jews. The same reluctance can sometimes be seen today in the choice of members of corporate boards:

> Even today some of the corporations founded by Jews would prefer to reduce the number of Jewish directors on their boards. As one of the men we interviewed said of his board:
> "It's about half Jewish. I'm making every effort to change it as rapidly as I can away from being a Jewish company. It just happened that way. You know we were a small company and went public and the board members were friends of my father's. That's the normal thing. Over the years we got more and more outside directorships. But when we look at new directors now, it's a negative thing if you're Jewish. I'm not saying we don't do it but it's a negative thing, it's more of a plus to be non-Jewish. I think it's bad for our company to have any image as a Jewish company."
> (Zweigenhaft and Domhoff, 1982, pp. 29–30)

In other words, there are exceptions to the idea that a company with a Jewish history will be more equitable to Jewish managers. One reason for this may be that the Jewish family members involved have internalized the view of Jews as outsiders in American society, a process we will examine more fully in a later chapter. Yet, on the average, it is clear that—consistent with the outsider hypothesis—there is a greater likelihood that Jews will be able to attain senior executive positions in companies with Jewish family backgrounds than in the far, far greater number of companies and industries without such Jewish backgrounds.

Conclusions

Perhaps the best way to summarize our analyses of the lack of Jewish representation at the executive level in such major segments of corporate America as those we have described here is with the phrase "The more things change, the more they stay the same." In 1959, in *The Power Elite,* C. Wright Mills wrote:

> The business executives are predominantly Protestant and more likely, in comparison with the proportions of the population at large, to be Episcopalians or Presbyterians than Baptists or Methodists. The Jews and Catholics among them are fewer than among the population at large.

In 1968, Lundberg wrote in *The Rich and the Super-Rich* that Jews were very underrepresented in corporate management compared to their frequency in the population and among college graduates. In 1972, Domhoff wrote that Jews, despite their business successes, were on the fringes of an Anglo-Saxon power elite centered on control of commercial banking, insurance, public utilities, and manufacturing, which for the most part excluded Jews.

And in 1983, a writer for a Washington newspaper reported:

> In a study at the Harvard School of Business Administration, more than 75 percent of business executives felt a Jewish religious background was a handicap to obtaining upper-level executive positions, so Jews are discouraged from seeking them, the commission said. . . .
>
> "Consequently, industry officials erroneously concluded that Jews are not really interested in such jobs and continue practices that have the effect of excluding them," according to the report. "Whatever their genesis, these practices have resulted in a virtual lockout of Jews from high-level positions in the business sector and have coalesced to create a self-perpetuating cycle of discrimination," the commission said. (Cunningham, 1983, p. A5)

There is little in the data we gathered in mid-1985 to change any of these conclusions. The evidence for the paradox between Jewish American success in the entrepreneurial role and the absence of Jews from the majority of corporate America is as true today as it was three decades ago. The 6 to 8 percent figure which has been cited in some studies for the proportion of Jewish Americans at the senior executive level on an overall basis has not taken into account great variations in these figures among different industries. The 6 to 8 percent level (actually 5 to 8 percent here) more accurately describes only a small minority of industries. An overwhelming majority of American corporations (in terms of sales figures and employment levels) can be characterized as having proportions of Jewish managers far below the 6 to 8 percent level; a far smaller number of corporations have proportions of Jewish managers above the 6 to 8 percent level. The latter group of companies is also far smaller than the group that has a minimal proportion of Jewish executives. In understanding these discrepancies, a key factor appears to be the degree to which the founding of the company was influenced by a Jewish family and the extent to which such influence may still exist.

One question that was addressed only minimally in these analyses but appears to be worth comment concerns the "expected" levels of Jewish employment in a particular context. It may be argued that such levels are a function of how one defines the relevant labor market for a particular position or organization. For managerial/executive careers, the relevant labor market has increasingly been defined as the college-graduate population, which, on the national level, is 10 percent Jewish. However, this figure is considerably greater if we define the labor market in the context of particular geographic areas, such as New York or Los Angeles. For these reasons, the question of a particular "expected" figure for Jewish levels of employment (or for employment of any other group) has multiple answers, depending on the context. For these reasons, also, percentages such as a 5 to 8 percent level of Jewish employment in a particular setting—percentage which may be seen by some as a satisfactory or even higher than expected figure—may actually be a serious underrepresentation of the characteristics of the labor market as far as Jews are concerned, even in the small minority of cases in which this level of employment exists.

6
Contemporary Corporate
Patterns of Recruitment
and Selection

T he most direct way in which a corporation may show an interest in employing members of a particular group is to recruit where such individuals are likely to be found. If there are Jewish applicants available where a potential employer recruits and the proverbial all else being equal requirement is met in terms of selection standards, it is likely that the employer is willing to consider Jews for employment. However, if the recruiting is being done where few potential Jewish applicants are available, there may be reason to question whether the employer has any interest in employing Jews. This chapter provides further evidence for the outsider status of Jews by showing how, in the past, major corporate employers have avoided recruiting at colleges and universities where Jewish Americans constituted a sizable segment of the student body and how they continue to evidence such lack of interest today.

The Slavin and Pradt Studies
of Corporate Recruiting

One of the most comprehensive examinations of the recruiting practices of American corporations relative to potential and actual

Jewish applicants has been reported by Slavin and Pradt (1982). The data they present, much of which will be summarized here, is highly suggestive of a consistent pattern among major American corporate employers to avoid recruiting Jews for managerial and executive career paths. Although the research they report has a number of serious methodological problems (to be noted) and their data consist of observed statistical patterns rather than being based on the actual decision-making processes utilized by those making recruiting and selection decisions, the findings of Slavin and Pradt are nevertheless rather compelling and worthy of examination.

The methodological procedure used by Slavin and Pradt in determining the impact of the percentage of potential Jewish applicants at a school on corporate recruiting decisions was a rather straightforward two-stage process. The first step was to determine the proportion of Jewish undergraduates in the student bodies of a number of colleges. Once these figures were obtained, the second step was to compare them to the average number of recruiting visits to each college during the years 1972–74 by employers of varying size and from different industries. Among the employer groups studied and reported in separate analyses were the Fortune 100, the rest of the Fortune 500 (those ranking from 101 to 500), insurance companies, banking firms (including commercial and savings institutions), and the public utilities (both those in the top fifty and other companies in this industry that were not as large). In addition to these breakdowns, Slavin and Pradt also classified the colleges according to size and analyzed each of the groups separately (as well as analyzing all colleges as a group). The different-sized college subgroups were studied separately to correct for the possibility that the results obtained might be influenced by a tendency of corporate recruiters to go to large schools, where the proportions of Jewish students might be lower. If this were the case, the results would indicate a negative relationship between the proportion of Jewish enrollment and the frequency of corporate recruiting that would be a function not of the proportion of Jewish students at a school but instead of the likelihood that corporate recruiters would go to larger schools. Small colleges were defined as those with less than 5,000 enrollment at the time of the study, medium-sized colleges as those with an enrollment of 5,000 to 10,000, and large colleges as those with an enrollment greater than 10,000.

The major trends of the findings (presented in statistical form in appendix 6A) can be summarized as follows:

1. As would be expected, the greatest numbers of recruiting visits were made to the large colleges. It was also among this group of schools that the greatest discrepancies occurred between the number of visits to schools with few Jewish students and the number of visits to institutions with a significant number of Jewish students. The discrepant patterns were particularly clear after the schools were classified into two groups: those in which more than 30 percent of the undergraduates were Jewish and those in which less than 30 percent were Jewish. Far more visits were made to schools in which Jews were less than 30 percent of the student body than to schools in which they were a larger proportion. For the Fortune 100 companies, three to five times as many visits were made to the schools with fewer Jewish students; for the banking industry, it was two and one-half to three times as many; and for some of the public utility firms, the ratio was as high as ten to one. The only exception to this pattern was the insurance industry, for which the trends were in the same direction but rather weak. One reason for this difference in industry patterns may be the tendency, noted earlier, for insurance companies to hire Jewish sales representatives to deal with an expected Jewish clientele.

2. Despite the fewer visits overall to the smaller schools and the decreased opportunity for discrepancies to occur, the same differential recruiting patterns occurred at these institutions. The pattern of fewer visits to schools with a greater than 30 percent Jewish student body is clear. Depending on the schools and the industry involved, the differences are two, three, and four times as great—in one or two cases, even more. One industry in which the differential recruiting patterns are particularly great is the public utilities, an industry we have already noted as one that has rarely had Jews at the senior executive level.

3. Since the average number of visits to schools in which the percentage of Jewish students is 30 percent or higher is consistently

far lower than it is for any other category of schools—either when colleges are grouped overall or when they are classified according to enrollment—Slavin and Pradt suggest that a 30 percent level of Jews in the undergraduate student body may be the "tipping point" at which corporate tendencies to avoid recruiting at a particular school become greatest.

Despite the consistency of these results, however, the methods used by Slavin and Pradt have to be considered before we come to any firm conclusions. One potential problem is that the authors do not provide us with the actual number of schools that fall into the small, medium, or large categories. Thus, we have little idea of the reliability of the findings in terms of sample sizes. Another problem is that no statistical tests of differences are provided for any of these analyses (although statistical analyses are used elsewhere in their research).

Though regrettable, these weaknesses are not fatal, and the authors do provide us with some additional information that supports their general conclusions. The authors state that they received responses from 128 schools out of 170 questionnaires sent out, and they do report the Jewish enrollment of these schools at the time of the study, though not total enrollments. Of the responding schools, 109 were in the 10 percent or under category, 19 were in the 10 to 19.9 percent group, 17 were in the 20 to 29.9 percent category, 11 were in the 30 to 39.9 percent group, and 11 had Jewish enrollments of 40 percent or more. Thus, there are a considerable number of schools in each group, particularly when the 30 to 39.9 percent and the 40 + percent groups are combined. However, it should be noted that the percentage of Jewish undergraduates in a school appears to be related to total enrollment, but in an apparently nonlinear fashion. For example, there are very large schools in the under 10 percent group (for example, the Universities of Texas, Washington, and Oklahoma) as well as in the significant (30 percent or more) category (for example, the colleges of the City University of New York, New York University, Boston University, and Temple University). In other words, large schools could be classified in either the over or under 30 percent groups. The same is not true of the smaller schools. Although many of the smaller schools had less than 10 percent Jewish enrollment, few of this group had more than 30 percent. This asymmetry suggests that the findings summarized in appendix 6A can be considered more trustworthy for the medium and larger schools than for the smaller institutions. These differences in the reliability of the data are not a problem for us, however, since it is at the larger schools (where the reliability is greatest) that the reluctance to interview at schools with significant Jewish enrollments showed up most clearly. Hence, there is no need to modify the conclusions made earlier.

Our general argument is enhanced even further when we control for the possible confounding factor of urban as opposed to rural campus settings. The potential problem here concerns the possibility of a Jewish preference for urban institutions and, conversely, a possible corporate preference for recruiting at rural campus schools. If such contradictory preferences exist, one might argue that the lack of recruitment at schools where there are significant numbers of Jewish students is more a function of corporate reluctance to recruit at urban institutions than an unwillingness to recruit where there are Jewish students. Although there is no direct test of this possibility in Slavin and Pradt's data, another analysis they report is relevant to the issue and suggests that it does not appear to be a viable explanation for the recruiting patterns they found. As table 6–1 shows, if we limit ourselves to companies that have recruited in the New York area (thus entirely eliminating the rural factor), there is still a considerable reluctance to recruit at schools where there are Jewish students.

Might the results of appendix 6A and table 6–1 be accounted for by some other factor? Might random variance be a possible explanation, either totally or in part? Slavin and Pradt provide us with a statistically rigorous answer to the latter possibility by developing and applying a probability model designed to assess the likelihood that a company would have chosen, purely on a random basis, out of the total number of schools it could choose to recruit at, to recruit at no school with more than 30 percent Jewish undergraduates, one school with more than 30 percent Jewish undergraduates, two schools with more than 30 percent Jewish undergraduates, and so forth. Their answer to the hypothesis that random variance could be an explanation for the recruiting choices of some very well

Table 6–1
Recruiting Visits in the New York Area, 1972–73

	No. of Visits	
Type of Company	Schools with > 30% Jewish Enrollment	Schools with < 30% Jewish Enrollment
Oil	1	52
Equipment	1	51
Food	1	44
Space	3	61
Copper	1	35
Technology	1	32
Oil	1	28
Steel	1	28
Construction	0	22
Retailing	2	40
Technology	0	20
Chemical	4	60
Retailing	4	60
Chemical	1	22
Paper	1	19

Source: S. L. Slavin and M. A. Pradt, *The Einstein Syndrome; Corporate Anti-Semitism in America Today* (Lanham, Md.: University Press of America, 1982, pp. 87–88.

known companies is "not very likely" (as shown in appendix 6B, which summarizes the findings). There are more than forty companies in their analysis—all major recruiters and among America's largest corporations—whose recruiting choice patterns could not be accounted for on the basis of a random model (using normally accepted levels of statistical significance). In brief, the differential recruiting patterns in favor of greater frequency of visits to schools with fewer numbers of Jewish students appear more likely to be accountable for by systematic, not random, factors. The significance of these findings is increased even further if we note the industries represented by the companies in appendix 6B. Particularly prominent there are companies from petroleum refining and related industries, the chemicals industry, the groups of industries that fall generally into metals manufacturing and refining, and the food industry. These industries are notable on several counts: their size and power relative to others, as measured by their rankings in the Fortune 500, and the already-noted lack of a Jewish presence at their senior executive levels in the mid-1980s.

In addition to their recruiting research, Slavin and Pradt also report two studies of corporate selection that are relevant to our concerns here. One of these investigations involved studying college alumni newsletters in order to determine the selection ratios for Jews and non-Jews at schools where both are enrolled and where recruitment is occurring. Who gets the job offers? Their analyses suggest that the selection ratios were indeed different for Jews and non-Jews. Given mixed applicant pools, non-Jews were more likely to be selected than Jews. Furthermore, a separate analysis showed that the discrepancy between corporate employment of alumni from colleges with low and high levels of Jewish enrollment was even greater when non-Jewish alumni from colleges with high levels of Jewish enrollment and Jewish alumni from colleges with low levels of Jewish enrollment were both eliminated from consideration. In other words, the development of "clear non-Jewish" and "clear Jewish" college groups made the differential selection ratios and the lower levels of Jewish employment even more apparent. Similar differences in selection ratios and discrepancies in employment patterns were identified when Jewish and non-Jewish graduates from the same college were compared. In my own college (Baruch College), which at the time of the study was 47 percent Jewish, it was found that of thirty graduates employed by the top 100 of the Fortune 500 companies, only three were Jewish. (If the likelihood of employment, or the selection ratio, were equally likely across different groups, one would have expected approximately fourteen Jews to have been so employed.) The figures for Baruch College graduates employed by other employers were also discrepant with an equal-likelihood selection model. For example, the proportion was eight (instead of an expected 13) Jews of twenty-seven employed by the Fortune 101 to 500, one of eight for those employed by the insurance industry (instead of an expected 4) and three of twenty-one for the banking industry (instead of an expected 10).

As this review indicates, most of the results reported by Slavin and Pradt are similar to the descriptive research reviewed earlier, which was concerned with the presence or absence of Jews in particular occupational settings. Hence, although conscious anti-Semitism might have contributed to the development of some of the patterns reported, the lack of direct information supporting such an inference suggests some caution in arguing for this type of explanation. Such caution is not necessary, however, when a study focuses on direct evidence of discriminatory attitudes and/or behavior.

Slavin and Pradt report such evidence and make the appropriate inferences in a study of executive recruiters (or headhunters, as they are sometimes called). In many respects, executive recruiters are at the cutting edge of the process involved in selecting top-level executives, since it is their business to know whom corporate leaders truly wish to employ in significant positions (as compared to what they might say for public relations purposes). A survey of the views of executive recruiters on the role of anti-Semitism in corporate selection could thus be very useful if the respondents were truly willing to share their experience. Unfortunately, Slavin and Pradt's investigation goes only part of the way toward meeting these needs; they received only 124 answers from an original sample of 373, and we have no idea how those who responded differed from those who did not. Yet even with this weakness, the study does provide us with some useful information, particularly since it presents explicit data on the expressed unwillingness to hire or consider Jews in executive selection. The results show directly and clearly that the fact of being Jewish is perceived as having a significant negative impact on consideration for managerial/executive positions. Sixteen recruiters said that they had received job orders specifically requesting non-Jews; twenty indicated that they would not send a Jewish applicant to some of the firms with which they work; twenty-seven indicated that Jews were less likely than non-Jews to get jobs in the banking industry; eighteen said that Jews were less likely to be hired in the large industrial companies; and twenty-three said that Jews were less likely to be hired by the oil companies.

The Slavin and Pradt studies constitute a comprehensive series of investigations into college recruiting and selection patterns related to Jews as such patterns were engaged in by American corporations during the early to mid 1970s. They deal with a number of issues and a number of different aspects of organizational recruitment and selection, and in this sense they are useful. The problem, however, is that they are also unfortunately marked by a rather sloppy presentation, a failure to use statistical tests of significance when they would have been appropriate, and an almost cavalier lack of attention to details normally relevant to research investigations, such as a description of procedures and sample size for a particular analysis.

Yet taken in context and despite these flaws, Slavin and Pradt's work provides compelling evidence that a significant number of American corporate employers systematically avoid potential Jewish employees in recruitment and selection decisions. Their evidence assumes even greater value when one considers that the alternative explanations explored and evaluated by the authors are not viable. On the positive side, also, the data are consistent in their implications, and the authors provide us with statistical control analyses in some instances that strengthen their case further. For these reasons, it would appear justifiable to conclude from the work of Slavin and Pradt that they have made an effective case for the presence of an apparently strong reluctance to consider and hire Jews in the college recruitment and selection practices of many American corporations during the first half of the 1970s.

Recruiting in the 1980s: A Follow-Up Analysis

A legitimate issue concerning the Slavin and Pradt research is that the data are over a decade old. What would happen if such research were done today? Would the results be the same, better, or worse? Is there any sign that Jews' outsider status in corporate America may be coming to an end, at least in terms of college recruiting practices?

As a partial response to these questions, I conducted a study of corporate recruiting patterns during the years 1983–86 at universities that could be matched along relevant academic dimensions but differed significantly in the proportion of Jewish students in their undergraduate enrollment (as listed in *Jewish Life on Campus*, published in 1985 by the B'nai B'rith Hillel Foundation, Washington, D.C.). The following schools were chosen for analysis:

1. Emory University, a privately supported university in the Southeast, listed as having 3,500 undergraduates, of whom 1,800 (slightly better than 50 percent) were Jewish

2. Vanderbilt University, a privately supported university, also in the Southeast, listed as having 4,000 undergraduates, of whom 200 (5 percent) were Jewish

3. University of Notre Dame, a Catholic institution in the Midwest that is not listed in the B'nai B'rith book but has been estimated to have fewer than 1 percent Jews in its undergraduate student body of approximately 7,500

4. Brandeis University, a privately supported university in the Northeast under Jewish sponsorship, listed as having 2,850 undergraduates, of whom approximately 2,000 (68 percent) were Jewish

5. Oberlin College, a privately supported college in the Midwest, listed as having 2,800 undergraduates, of whom 1,200 (43 percent) were Jewish

6. Tufts University, a privately supported university in the Northeast, listed as having 4,500 undergraduates, of whom 1,800 (40 percent) were Jewish

Among the characteristics of these institutions are the following:

1. All are selective institutions and are reasonably comparable to one another in terms of median student SAT scores. According to the Barron's 1985 handbook, these scores were as follows:

	Verbal	Mathematics
Emory	550	600
Vanderbilt	550	600
Notre Dame	560	630
Brandeis	580	610
Oberlin	600	616
Tufts	575	632

2. Three pairs of institutions are in similar areas of the country (Emory and Vanderbilt are in the Southeast, Brandeis and Tufts are in the Northeast, and Notre Dame and Oberlin are in the Midwest).

3. Recruiting patterns could be compared explicitly for cases in which companies listed themselves as interested in the types of college graduates who were also available from the other institutions. In most cases, this meant comparing corporate recruiters that specifically listed themselves with the respective college recruiting offices as interested in liberal arts/computer sciences/business majors or, in two cases, engineering majors. Companies that were interested in graduate students or in students with majors not available in the other institutions for which comparisons were being made were not considered in the analysis.

In sum, Emory and Tufts are fine private universities with a number of different undergraduate schools and a significant percentage of Jewish students; Vanderbilt and Notre Dame are fine private universities with few Jewish undergraduates; and Brandeis and Oberlin are fine, basically liberal arts institutions with a significant Jewish undergraduate student body. The results of the survey and the relevant comparisons were as follows:

1. A total of six Fortune 100 companies recruited at Emory during 1983–84 for students in business, computer sciences, and liberal arts; twenty companies from the same group recruited in the same areas at Vanderbilt during the following academic year. The latter group included companies from such industries as petroleum, chemicals, and automobile manufacturing, none of which recruited at Emory. So far as could be determined, there were no radical business changes one year later that would account for such a difference. Furthermore, year-to-year changes in the economy would not account for the fact that during the same year that six Fortune 100 companies recruited at Emory, forty-five such companies recruited at Notre Dame, while only one recruited at Brandeis and four recruited at Oberlin the following year.

2. A comparison of recruiting patterns at Vanderbilt and Tufts, schools very similar to one another in size and structure and both with schools of engineering, showed that a total of forty-three Fortune 100 companies visited the former, while only ten recruited at the latter.

3. Consistent with the general conclusion that historical patterns may not have changed very much from those noted earlier in

Table 6–2
Recruiting Patterns in the Mid-1980s

Fortune Group	Number of Recruiting Visits					
	Emory	Vanderbilt	Notre Dame	Brandeis	Oberlin	Tufts
1–20	0	10	13	1	2	1
21–40	3	13	11	0	1	5
41–60	1	8	8	0	1	2
61–80	2	9	6	0	0	2
81–100	0	3	7	0	0	0

this book is that several of the largest commercial banks in the New York area were listed as recruiting at Notre Dame, approximately 750 miles from New York, as were two of the largest utilities in the New York area (one of which later canceled). None of these employers were listed as recruiting at schools with significant numbers of Jewish students.

Some of these differences are seen in table 6–2, which shows that there were eighty-eight recruiting visits to Vanderbilt and Notre Dame, which had a combined undergraduate enrollment of approximately 11,500 and Jewish enrollments of 1 percent and 5 percent, respectively. Together, these institutions include colleges of liberal arts, business administration, and engineering. These figures contrast with a total of twenty-one recruiting visits for the other four schools, which have high levels of Jewish enrollment. These four schools have a total enrollment of approximately 10,000 and also include colleges of liberal arts, business administration, and engineering.

It would appear that although more evidence is needed regarding the cognitive and attitudinal processes that underlie actual corporate recruiting decisions, there is little reason to believe that things have changed very much in the decade since Slavin and Pradt's data were collected. Since early in the 1970s and continuing to the present, the available evidence shows that college recruiters from large segments of corporate America are far more likely to go to schools where there are few Jewish undergraduates than they are to go to schools where Jews are a significant part of the undergraduate student body.

Appendix 6A:
Average Number of Recruiting Visits of Different Types of Companies to Campuses of Varying Size and with Varying Jewish Enrollments, 1972–74

Percentage of Jewish Undergrads	Number of Visits			
	Total	Small Colleges[a]	Medium Colleges[b]	Large Colleges[c]

I. Fortune 500 Companies

Percentage of Jewish Undergrads	Top 100	Next 400	Top 100	Next 400	Top 100	Next 400	Top 100	Next 400
Under 10	20.0	19.8	8.9	7.7	17.9	13.9	31.5	34.6
10–19.9	21.9	22.2	6.4	6.8	23.8	17.5	40.0	42.1
20–29.9	19.0	15.8	14.7	10.4	15.5	17.5	31.3	29.3
30–39.9	13.6	9.2	7.4	4.7	11.5	6.8	10.0	8.4
40+	4.3	3.5	—[d]		—[d]		—[d]	

II. Insurance Companies

Percentage of Jewish Undergrads	Total	Small Colleges	Medium Colleges	Large Colleges
Under 10	10.5	7.6	10.3	13.0
10–19.9	9.6	7.6	12.0	10.6
20–29.9	7.8	6.3	11.5	10.0
30–39.9	8.6	6.8	8.3	10.1
40+	7.5			

III. Banks[e]

Percentage of Jewish Undergrads	Total	Small Colleges	Medium Colleges	Large Colleges
Under 10	6.8	5.7	9.3	9.3
10–19.9	5.7	5.8	5.6	5.6
20–29.9	9.3	10.0	8.3	8.3
30–39.9	5.2	4.4	3.8	3.8
40+	3.5			

IV. Fortune Top 50 Public Utilities

Percentage of Jewish Undergrads	Total	Small Colleges	Medium Colleges	Large Colleges
Under 10	1.9	0.8	1.7	3.1
10–19.9	3.5	1.9	1.6	6.4
20–29.9	2.1	1.4	3.5	2.7
30–39.9	1.2	0.4	0.8	1.3
40+	0.4			

V. Other Public Utilities

Percentage of Jewish Undergrads	Total	Small Colleges	Medium Colleges	Large Colleges
Under 10	1.9	0.7	2.1	3.0
10–19.9	2.3	1.4	1.3	4.0
20–29.9	0.9	1.0	1.0	0.7
30–39.9	0.4	0.2	0.3	0.3
40+	0.1			

Source: S. L. Slavin and M. A. Pradt, *The Einstein Syndrome: Corporate Anti-Semitism in America Today* (Lanham, Md.: University Press of America, 1982), pp. 50, 53, 54, 55.

[a]Colleges with enrollments 5000 or below.

[b]Colleges with enrollments between 5001 to 10,000.

[c]Colleges with enrollments greater than 10,000.

[d]Because of smaller sample sizes when colleges are classified according to enrollment size, the breakdowns according to Jewish enrollment are presented in three categories.

[e]The analysis in this category included other types of banking institutions besides commercial banks, e.g. savings banks, mutual savings banks, and savings and loan associations.

Appendix 6B:
Recruiting Patterns of American Corporations, 1972–73

Company	Number of Colleges Visited	Probability of Random Avoidance
Group I: Visited No Colleges with 30% Jewish Undergrads		
Goodyear	55	.0002
PPG	55	.0002
Schlumberger Well Service	48	.0005
Shell Oil	38	.0034
Armco Steel	34	.0066
Borg-Warner	34	.0066
Amoco Chemicals	30	.0127
Square "D"	29	.0149
Ethyl Corporation	27	.0205
Alcoa	26	.0240
Cities Service	25	.0281
Union Oil	25	.0281
Oscar Mayer	24	.0328
U.S. Gypsum	23	.0383
Deere	22	.0446
George A. Hormel	22	.0446
Phillips Petroleum	22	.0446
Turner Construction Co.	22	.0446
American Air Filter	21	.0519
Fluor Corp.	21	.0519
National Steel	21	.0519
Whirlpool	21	.0519
Group II: Visited One College with 30% Jewish Undergrads		
Monsanto	54	.0009
Continental Oil	52	.0013
Babcock and Wilcox	51	.0015
Motorola	48	.0024
Allis Chalmers	45	.0038
Diamond Shamrock	44	.0045
Dow	44	.0045
Stauffer	44	.0045
General Motors	40	.0081
Anaconda	36	.0141
Eaton	36	.0141
Union Oil	36	.0141
Chicago Bridge and Iron	33	.0210
Ingersoll Rand	32	.0238
Jones and Laughlin	31	.0270
Republic Steel	29	.0345
Boeing	28	.0389
U.S. Steel	28	.0389
Carnation	27	.0437
FMC	27	.0437
NCR	27	.0437
Gulf Oil	26	.0490
Owens Corning	26	.0490

Source: S. L. Slavin and M.A. Pradt, *The Einstein Syndrome: Corporate Anti-Semitism in America Today* (Lanham, Md.: University Press of America, 1982), pp. 65, 67, 72, 74.

7
Jews, the Professions, and Corporate America: Another Success Story

The professions have been significant paths to career success for the minority of American Jews who have had the ability, the motivation, and the financial resources to qualify for these occupations. A major reason for such success has been the similarity between the professional and entrepreneurial roles as they have developed in the American culture. As with the need for entrepreneurs, the explosive growth and success of the American business system generated an increasing demand for professional assistance, both in and out of the work setting, and also provided the financial resources to support such assistance. Similarly, as with the entrepreneurial role, the self-controlled nature and portability of the professional role caused it to be seen as concordant with Jewish values and particularly attractive to those who were and continued to believe themselves to be an outsider group in American society.

There has been one major difference, however, between the experiences of Jewish aspirants to managerial/executive career paths and those of Jewish professionals: Jewish professionals have also been utilized by corporate America, particularly in recent years, in professional and staff positions and as consultants. A major reason for this pattern, which is consistent with the view of Jews as outsiders in corporate America, is that social acceptability is far less crucial in the performance of professional responsibilities than it is for managerial/executive career success. Intellectual competence and technical knowledge are far more important determinants of success for professionals than for managers, and outsider status is perceived as significantly less important for professionals than for those aspiring to managerial/executive vertical career mobility.

Overall, then, the occupational picture has generally been far brighter for Jews who are professionals than for those who are managerial/executive career aspirants. There is a cloud on the horizon, however; for reasons to be detailed later, there is an increasing likelihood of fewer career possibilities for professionals in the not too distant future. As a result, managerial/executive career path possibilities and the factors that may be affecting them are assuming increasing salience for all career-oriented Americans, non-Jewish and Jewish.

The Partially Closed Gates prior to World War II: Elite Colleges, Professional Schools, and the Quota System

In the years prior to World War II, quotas were commonly used in controlling the number of Jews who would be admitted both to the elite colleges that, to a great extent, controlled entry into professional schools and to the professional schools themselves. Typical of such procedures were the discriminatory practices used by Harvard and Yale on the undergraduate level and by such important medical schools as those at Columbia and Cornell.

In 1922 the two most prestigious American universities, Harvard and Yale, began to put into practice quota systems that eventually limited Jewish applicants in both schools to about 10 percent of the available student places. In the most publicized of these cases, then President A. Lawrence Lowell of Harvard University called for an admission quota for Jewish students—a call that legitimated and made public what had been an open secret at American universities for years. Now, however, the situation was different, for the head of the most prestigious American scholarly institution had gone public with a proposal that Jews should not be treated like other Americans but, rather, should have their admission limited, regardless of their qualifications and regardless of their competence. According to President Lowell, a quota was necessary because the acceptance of too many Jews would lead to negative consequences for both Jews and non-Jews—or so he argued. In his view, the utilization of quotas for restricting Jewish students would be partially for the Jewish students' own good.

Lowell's proposals caused a storm among the Harvard alumni and student body, in the Massachusetts legislature, and in the nation at large. It was one thing for a quota to be used informally, without public acknowledgment, by lesser schools; it was something else for Harvard University to make such an open statement of its intent to engage in religious discrimination. The eventual result of the furor was that a faculty commission at Harvard rejected the concept of explicit religious quotas but opened the possible alternative of regional quotas—a procedure that, to all intents and purposes, had a similar effect of reducing Jewish enrollment, at least for a while. It was not until years later that the regional quota system was done away with by Harvard President James Bryant Conant in the interests of a merit system of selection.

Less publicized over the years than the controversy at Harvard were the policies followed by Yale University. Yet the situations and the views were apparently quite similar, as evidence that has recently come to light has indicated:

Not until the early 1960's did Yale University end an informal admissions policy that restricted Jewish enrollment to about 10 percent, according to a new book published by Yale University Press.

The book, "Joining the Club," which began as a sophomore term paper by Dan A. Oren, a 1979 Yale graduate, documents antisemitism reaching from fraternity brothers to board trustees. Much of the research is based on university documents.

One document, a folder now in the university archives, labeled "Jewish Problem," contains a memo from the admissions chairman of 1922 urging limits on the "alien and unwashed element". The next year, the admissions committee enacted the "Limitations of Numbers" policy, an informal quota. Jewish enrollment was held to about 10 percent for four decades.

"There were vicious, ugly forms of discrimination at Yale, as with the larger society," the current Yale University Secretary, John A. Wilkinson, said. "It's part of our history, and we should face up to it."

This book, he said, has uncovered "what we've all suspected and some have known for a long time."

The restrictive policy was phased out beginning in 1960 when the Yale President, A. Whitney Griswold, issued directives stating that an applicant's religion should have no place in the admissions process. (Johnson, 1986, pp. B1, B5)

From a historical perspective, these events of the early 1920s at Harvard and Yale had enormous impact. The legitimation of quotas by these schools strengthened the use of similar procedures among less significant collegiate institutions, with the result that such constraints on Jewish enrollment remained part of the American scene for years. One of the more famous incidents illustrating the continuing use of such quotas took place in 1945 when, even with all the horrors of World War II still fresh in people's minds, the then-president of Dartmouth College defended a quota system for Jewish students at his institution, since, to quote him, "Dartmouth is a Christian college founded to Christianize its students."

The institution of these quotas is important in understanding the nature of the professions in the United States at that time and the manner in which individuals gained access to such occupations. In brief, elite colleges such as Harvard, Yale, and Dartmouth were significant passageways to professional schools—particularly in the Northeast, where most of the Jewish population lived at that time— and it was because of their status that the quota systems of these colleges had such an impact on the likelihood of Jews' gaining entrance to the professions. A further complication for Jewish professional aspirants during this era was that such quota systems were not limited to undergraduate institutions. There were also admissions quotas for the professional schools themselves:

By the mid-1930's half the students applying to American medical schools were Jews. In no branch of higher education, however, was anti-Semitism quite so virulent or restrictive quotas so high; as a result, Jews constituted only 17 percent of those admitted to American medical schools. Those who could afford to do so attended medical school in Europe (ironically, Jews were more welcome at the medical schools of Mussolini's Italy than in the United States). But nearly six out of seven Jewish applicants had to abandon their ambition, and untold others did not bother to apply to medical schools at all; some became pharmacists or dentists instead. In Stamford, Connecticut, in 1938, for example, there were as many Jewish dentists as there were doctors; Jews of that era used to joke that "D.D.S." after one's name stood for "disappointed doctor or surgeon." (Silberman, 1985, p. 124)

A famous illustration of how this discrimination operated in New York in 1940 was when Dean W.S. Ladd (of Cornell Medical School in New York City) explained to City Councilman Walter R. Hart: "We limit the number of Jews . . . to roughly the proportion of Jews . . . in this state, which is a higher proportion than in any part of the country" (Belth, 1979). (This statement was in response to questions asked because of figures indicating that out 1,200 applicants to Cornell Medical School (of whom 700 were Jewish) only 10 of the 80 eventually admitted were Jews. A Jewish applicant's chance of admission was thus one in seventy, while among non-Jews it was one in seven.)

After the Gates Opened: Post–World War II

After the end of World War II, many of the discriminatory admission practices fell by the wayside. The professions became, even more, a major avenue for upward career mobility and financial security for Jewish Americans who had the appropriate ability, motivation, and financial resources. The doors to professional careers swung open wider, and even though discrimination still existed in some quarters, there was still considerable opportunity available for those who were qualified. In the late 1950s, when Jews still faced difficulties in obtaining professional career opportunities, approximately 17 percent of all law students were Jewish (when Jews were 3 percent of the population), even though the students were aware of the considerable level of anti-Semitism existing at the time:

One pertinent study focused on Jewish and gentile graduates from an Ivy League law school that prepares students for elite positions. In the period from 1951 to 1962, among those who subsequently obtained jobs in New York City, Jewish graduates were at a substantial disadvantage in the job market. Compared to gentiles, Jewish graduates were significantly less likely to obtain one of their first three job choices and were also more likely to earn a lower starting salary. . . . 45 per cent of Jewish students at the four law schools studied had a job secured upon graduation. This figure is compared to 57 per cent of the Catholics and 76 per cent of the Protestants who said, as graduation approached, that they had a job waiting for them. . . .

On the one hand, Jews enter the profession in large numbers and, as best we know, eventually find employment as often as do others. On the other hand, Jews who aspire to careers in the large and more prestigious law firms are likely to encounter rebuff. . . .

Considering this record it is hardly surprising that Jewish law students were aware of discrimination in their chosen profession. Even much earlier, upon entering law school, 38 per cent of the Jewish students already said their religion would "make it somewhat harder for me to get into the things I'm interested in" in their career as a lawyer. Such feelings occurred very rarely among Protestants and Catholics—1 per cent and 8 per cent respectively. By the end of the third year, as graduation approached and students were about to begin their careers, the belief among Jewish students that they would encounter discrimination rose to 50 per cent. (Goldberg, 1970, pp. 150, 152)

Despite these problems, the decades since World War II have been good years for those Jews who have been able to qualify. Jews have been able to enter professional, scientific, and intellectual careers in large numbers, making these occupations a success story for American Jewry and for the nation as a whole.

Both statistical analyses and journalistic case studies have shown that Jews have benefited from the increasing opportunities available to them in these careers. One indication of such success can be seen by estimates of the percentages of individuals in various professions who identify themselves as Jewish. Landau (1984) provides one set of such estimates:

Medicine	6.9%
Specialized medicine	9.2%
Psychiatry	14.3%
Dentistry	9.0%
Law	8.0%
Mathematics professors	8.5%
Architecture	5.1%
Engineering	3.3%

It should be noted that these figures are only estimates, and their sources are not presented. Some analysts have suggested even higher percentages, at least for some professions. For example, Krefetz (1982) suggests that as many as one-fifth of the lawyers in this country are Jewish, as are approximately 30 percent of the psychiatric/clinical psychology professionals. Others present slightly different figures (see Silberman, 1985). Clearly, Jews in this country have been successful in virtually all of the professions considerably beyond their proportion in the American population (2.5 to 3 percent) and in some cases even beyond their proportion in the college graduate population (10 percent).

Consistent with Jews' success in such applied professions as medicine and law has been their success in professions involving academic/intellectual pursuits. In virtually all areas of intellectual activity—that is, the hard and soft sciences and the humanities—Jews have made major contributions. In reviewing Kadushin's research on the prominence of American Jews in intellectual circles, Silberman (1985) noted findings indicating that 24 percent of those who published twenty or more articles were Jewish and that one-half of 200 American academic elite were Jewish, as were 20 percent of the faculties in elite institutions (as opposed to 10 percent of college faculty members overall). In research involving even more highly prestigious intellectually oriented competition, Prager and Telushkin (1983) reported that one-quarter of the Nobel-prize-winning American scientists have been Jews. These awards have been given to Jews in such diverse areas as medicine and physiology (for example, Selman Waksman, Rosalyn Yalow, Joseph Goldstein, and Michael Brown), economics (for example, Paul Samuelson,

Kenneth Arrow, Lawrence Klein, and Milton Friedman), and literature (for example, Saul Bellow and Isaac Singer). In a separate
analysis, I found that an estimated 22 percent of the recipients of
eighty-nine Distinguished Scientific Contribution Awards from the
American Psychological Association (1985) since 1956 were members of the Jewish faith.

Also important to note are contributions by Jews to socially
significant concerns, such as the women's movement in this country. Although few such individuals have been employed in the academic world in terms of university appointments, they have been
among the more important influences—political, intellectual and
otherwise. Jewish writers, lecturers, and political figures such as
Betty Freidan, Susan Weidman Schneider, Shulamith Firestone,
Bella Abzug, and Lettie Coffin Pogrebin are among those who have
been particularly prominent in the continuing ferment of ideas and
proposals that have marked the women's movement during the past
two decades.

The Jewish Professional
and Corporate America

The outsider hypothesis suggests that organizations select different
types of people for professional positions such as accounting, law,
computer programming, and human resource management than for
managerial/executive career paths. The reason for such differential
selection is that the requirements for the professions are more professional and technical capability and intellectual abilities than social interaction skills and social acceptability. Since these are work
areas that a considerable number of Jews have selected for their
careers and in which they have shown capability, we would expect
a far greater Jewish presence in the professions in corporate America than in managerial/executive roles. The evidence we have supports this expectation.

One type of evidence is anecdotal—information that is usually
interesting and enlightening in an emotional sense but is rarely systematic and is almost always open to other types of interpretations.
Nevertheless, there is considerable anecdotal information that sup-

ports the conclusion of a greater Jewish corporate presence in the professions than in managerial/executive career paths. Some of this evidence is found in the research by Slavin and Pradt (1982), discussed in the preceding chapter. These authors cite many illustrations of the employment of Jews in corporate professional positions and refer to such hiring patterns as the operation of "the Einstein syndrome" in organizational selection. (In fact, *The Einstein Syndrome* is the title of their book.) Slavin and Pradt (1982) have noted:

> A very high proportion of data processing jobs is held by Jews—and Orientals, for that matter. Accounting positions, as well as those in law, personnel, public relations, economic analysis, and other highly technical fields are staffed largely by Jews. In fact, in few large corporations can one find Jews in anything *other* than these specialized staff positions. There is one exception, however—sales. Especially when the customers happen to be Jewish. . . . (p. 3)
>
> Like New York's other leading banks, Manufacturer's Hanover's Jewish officers are concentrated in "Jewish jobs"—factoring, legal work, computer programming and the like. . . . (p. 134)
>
> One disgruntled Jewish bank officer told us, "Jews can work in banks—as long as they don't get too close to the money." An indication of how Jews are treated is the allocation of jobs within the large New York banks. One officer at Irving Trust told us that Italians and Jews have traditionally been confined to operations rather than lending at most banks. Of the 50-odd Jewish bank officers we interviewed, all but three were either in computer programming, accounting, public relations, legal work, economic analysis, personnel, real estate, operations or factoring. (pp. 137–38)

Other researchers have made the same observations, but again in a relatively nonrigorous manner. Rottenberg (1979) discusses incidents at Anheuser-Busch and Exxon facilities in New Jersey where Jewish executives were finally hired after continuing complaints by the Anti-Defamation League about their lack of presence despite the location of the particular company units in an area of the country where Jews constituted a large proportion of the college-educa-

ted population. In both cases the executives hired were in profes-
sional/research positions, a pattern that Rottenberg points out did
not surprise the ADL officials involved.

Other evidence for these conclusions is found in the interviews
with managers and consultants reported in an earlier chapter. A
notable pattern in these interviews was the frequent citation by both
groups of the increased use of Jewish consultants by many firms in
recent years. Also, in the previously discussed research on recruiting
patterns in the 1980s, it was found that *all* of the accounting Big 8
CPA firms recruited at Emory, a school that had a large percentage
of Jewish undergraduates but at which only six of the Fortune 100
companies had recruited. In addition, in a study I conducted of
backgrounds of corporate board members, it was found in a random sample of thirty-eight of the top Fortune 100 firms that 19 of
44 Jewish board members were from academia, while only 17 of
the 155 non-Jewish board members were from academic settings
(proportionately, one-fourth as many). Assuming that an individual's background influences the reasons for selection, it would appear that the Jewish board members were likely to be chosen for
their academic rather than managerial skills, a pattern that was
much less true for the non-Jewish board members.

A Study of Industrial and Organizational
Psychology Professionals

Although the foregoing pattern supports the general conclusion that
Jews are more likely to be hired by corporate America for professional positions than for managerial/executive roles, the data presented are mostly anecdotal and are spread over a number of professions. This section presents a more systematic study I conducted
into the likelihood of employment of Jewish professionals by corporate America, focusing on the patterns for one profession—industrial and organizational (I-O) psychology.

As a profession, I-O psychology goes back to the turn of the
twentieth century, when Harvard psychologist Hugo Muensterberg
developed a test for selecting Boston streetcar conductors. Since
that time, and particularly since World War II, industrial and orga-

nizational psychology has expanded rapidly, both as an academic discipline and as a profession. Working in an applied setting—that is, an organization in either the private or the public sector—the I-O psychologist of today will utilize psychological theory, research findings, and techniques in varied ways to increase accuracy in personnel selection, to train and develop individuals and groups more effectively, to improve leadership quality, and to design jobs and work environments so as to increase the likelihood of effective performance and the degree to which workers' jobs and careers are a source of emotional well-being for them. Today, I-O psychology is an active, thriving profession that provides extremely valuable services to corporate America and to the individuals who work in the corporate setting. Among the individuals who provide these services are both non-Jewish and Jewish I-O psychologists. On the basis of two studies specifically conducted for our purposes, their patterns of work activity and employment suggest that they are indistinguishable from one another.

The first study consisted of a survey of the 1985–86 membership rolls of a professional association of applied I-O psychologists in a large northeastern city to determine ethnic background (Jewish or non-Jewish) and current occupational classification. In determining Jewish or non-Jewish background, the names method, described earlier, was the basic technique employed, but in this case there were follow-up calls and questioning of known friends of the individuals in cases where there were some doubts. After eliminating from consideration individuals who listed only home addresses without occupations and graduate students at local universities, occupations were classified into four categories: academic positions, corporate positions in the private sector, (full-time) consulting positions, and positions with governmental organizations.

According to our argument, we predicted that the occupational patterns of the Jewish and non-Jewish I-O psychologists should not be significantly different from one another. The results were fairly consistent with this prediction, as indicated in table 7–1.

Although there is some indication that organizations in the private sector are more likely to employ non-Jews than Jews—even in professional roles—the patterns are not greatly dissimilar, and it would be difficult to argue that Jewish industrial and organizational

Table 7–1

Employment Patterns for Jewish and Non-Jewish Industrial and Organizational Psychologists

Employment Area	Jews		Non-Jews	
	Number	*Percentage*	*Number*	*Percentage*
Academic	11	10	15	9
Corporate	48	43	86	49
Consulting	45	40	59	34
Government	8	7	15	9

psychologists have much difficulty gaining employment in corporate America, whether as full-time corporate employees or as consultants. The patterns suggest slightly greater difficulty, but probably no more than that.

The second study consisted of a small-scale replication of the first study, utilizing the membership rolls of a small association of I-O psychologists that required a special invitation for membership. There are a number of such groups in I-O psychology, as there are analogous groups in most professional fields, but the notable characteristic of this particular group was its attempt to balance its membership from both the academic and corporate/consulting (or more applied) spheres of the field. So far as could be determined, religious identity had played no role whatsoever in issuing invitations to membership. At the time of this study, there were twenty-one members in the group, seven of whom were Jewish.

Of relevance to us here is that the occupational classifications of the Jewish and non-Jewish members of this group were quite similar to one another. Of the seven Jewish psychologists, three were primarily involved with the corporate world and four were primarily academics with consulting activities on the side. Of the non-Jewish psychologists in this group, five were primarily from the corporate world and nine were academics. These figures are not different in any statistically significant manner, and they provide further support for our conclusion regarding the greater employability of Jews in the corporate world as professionals as opposed to managerial/executive positions.

The Impact of Professional Success:
Expected and Unexpected Effects

Significant levels of achievement in professional careers benefit both the individuals involved and the society in which they live and work. American society and its corporations have benefited greatly from the expertise and knowledge that Jewish professionals have contributed to those around them, but the individuals involved and the Jewish American community have also benefited. Besides the obvious benefits of the material wealth and social standing that typically inhere in the professional role and that enhance the self-image and social image of the individuals involved, the successful movement of members of the Jewish faith into the professions has enabled them to represent effectively and with a considerable degree of power (when they choose to exercise it) some of the major interests and concerns of the Jewish community. Such impact, real and potential, is not to be negated. Having representatives in powerful positions is crucially important to any group in a world where conflict and compromise between different group interests are an inherent part of everyday existence. This is no less true of the Jewish American community than it is of any other group.

Yet such benefits are not the whole story. It is an old maxim that there is a price to be paid for all benefits, and a closer examination of the success of Jews as professionals (and entrepreneurs) suggests that this has been the case here, also, and that we need to be aware of what this price has been. One such unintended effect of Jewish success in the self-controlled occupations has been to distract attention from several of the paradoxes we have noted in this book. It may be argued that the well-publicized success of a substantial segment of the Jewish community as entrepreneurs and in the professions has contributed to our lack of awareness of the absence of Jews from significant managerial roles in corporate America. Similarly, such success may also have distracted us from realizing that opportunities for entering professional roles are beginning to be limited as a result of affirmative action and similar programs that encourage differential recruitment and selection of minority groups (not including Jews) and for other reasons to be discussed later. In addition, it is also important to keep in mind that many of the professions (such as teaching) are not self-controlled but involve organizational employers, with all that that implies, and that three of four Jewish Americans are not professionals and that their conditions of work also need to be examined.

A Developing Problem: Declining Opportunities in the Professions

A problem facing all young Americans today, Jewish and non-Jewish, who may be interested in one of the professions as a possible career is the developing decline in opportunities in these ocupations. Among the reasons for this decline are a potential oversupply of trained individuals and changing technological/service delivery systems.

Oversupply of Trained Individuals

On September 7, 1987, an *International Herald Tribune* news item reported that the number of applicants to American medical schools had dropped 4.8 percent in 1986. According to the article, this was no accidental statistical blip—it was the fifth year in a row that a decline in applications to medical schools had occurred, and a further decline was expected in 1987.

The decline noted in this news item suggests an increasing public consciousness of a change in our professions that promises to have enormous impact on the career choices of many young Americans in coming generations.

> Organized medicine is seeking to limit the rapid growth in the supply of doctors, particularly specialists, which leaders in the profession say is making a dent in the substantial incomes most physicians receive.
>
> A report issued by the American Medical Association's board of trustees calls for doctors, states and education officials to review the size of medical school enrollments and urges standards that would limit the admission of foreign-trained doctors into the American medical system. . . .

> Physician supply is growing much faster than the general population. . . . Many parts of the country have a "surplus of physicians regardless of specialty", it said, and some specialists are in surplus "in most areas of the U.S." . . .
>
> Many physicians formerly boycotted health maintenance organizations, prepaid health plans in which doctors are paid set fees for their services. . . . "But today, . . . they are lining up seeking the opportunity to work in H.M.O.'s." . . .
>
> Partly because of the competition for patients, at least 25 percent of all doctors now work as employees of prepaid health plans, corporations or hospitals, rather than as independent practitioners. (Freudenheim, 1986, pp. 1, 15)

It is not just the medical profession that may be seeing an oversupply of trained individuals. It may be happening in other areas also. In recent years, our nation's law schools have sent between 35,000 and 40,000 new lawyers into the labor market each year, and we now have more than 100,000 individuals in this country who can be classified in the psychological professions (Stapp, Tucker, and VandenBos, 1985). Perhaps the output of lawyers may explain why applications to our nation's law schools declined 20 percent from 1982 to 1986, why 85 percent of these schools received fewer applications in 1985 than they did in 1984 (Evangelauf, 1986b), and why many law school deans are dissatisfied with the recruiting process for their graduates (Evangelauf, 1986a).

Are we graduating too many professionals? Are the increased advertisements and the TV and radio commercials for lawyers and plastic surgeons and professionals of all kinds a reaction to increased competition in overcrowded fields, or do they just reflect changing social norms? These questions are difficult to answer, but they must be answered, regardless of the complexities. The definition of an adequate supply of individuals in a profession is a function of cultural factors regarding the professional services that are perceived as necessary and/or desirable. Sometimes these factors are reflected in governmental funding patterns. Sometimes we can obtain direct access to the attitudes of the profession itself, in terms of the numbers of individuals it believes necessary in order to aid societal functioning.

There is also the issue of differentiating between the overall numbers of individuals in a profession and to their allocation among various subspecialties. In addition, there is the fact of cycles; job markets often lose their viability for a time and then, through retirement cycles and the like, pick up again in terms of opportunities. Professions that are overcrowded at one time may not be at another, and it takes time to train a professional adequately. One potential illustration of this cyclical process is college teaching in the humanities and social sciences; the field has had few opportunities in the late 1970s and through the 1980s, but the opportunities are likely to increase significantly in the 1990s as large numbers of these professionals who began their careers in the 1950s and 1960s begin to retire.

Yet given all these caveats—and they are important—there is little doubt that the oversupply in at least some professional areas has become a legitimate issue that has begun to affect the level and nature of some professional training in this country and the opportunities available to those entering the labor market.

Technological and Service Delivery Changes

Consider the following statistics from a recent article (Evangelauf, 1986c): From 1975 to 1985, there was a 60 percent decline in applications to dental school in this country; the number of applicants per dental school opening declined from 2.7 to 1.3. Estimates for the class entering in 1986 indicated a further decline in applications of 11 percent. First-year enrollment at the nation's dental schools is down 21 percent since 1978, and at least two universities (Oral Roberts University and Emory University) are planning to close down their D.D.S programs.

Dentistry is a major illustration of how some professions are changing as a result of changes in technology and service delivery systems. It was once a profession of great opportunity, but it is now characterized by the rapid growth of new methods of tooth and gum care that have decreased the frequency and level of dental services needed by millions of Americans. This is not to say that all dental treatment will become unnecessary (our aging population will need many types of dental care) but rather that the nature of the medical and treatment processes will change to such a degree that the dental profession as we know it today may not exist in a generation or two. With such changes, there will be changes in the kinds of career opportunities open to young Americans and the potential fruitfulness of dentistry as a career.

Dentistry is not the only field where there will be a decline in the number of needed professionals as a result of new technology and/or changes in service delivery methods. As mentioned earlier, the growth of new types of health care programs (for example, HMOs) is also leading to changes and predicted declines in the number of needed physicians. A recent study by a public health service team at Johns Hopkins University has shown that 1980 projections of the number of physicians needed in this country by the year 2000 may have overstated the mark by as much as 50 percent and that the new types of medical service delivery systems will reduce the need for physicians by as much as half (*Chronicle of Higher Education*, 1986).

8

Economic Motivation and Insider-Outsider Status

We generally act differently toward family members or those whom we consider insiders than toward those whom we consider outsiders. If other people are considered to be family members, economic motivation becomes less important. Our interactions with them are more likely to be based on affiliative considerations and on such human emotions as warmth, consideration, and the desire to meet their human needs. As most parents will tell you, the satisfactions derived from having children have little to do with profit and loss considerations in an economic sense. Few, if any, parents have ever been able to justify their decision to have children on the basis of financial values attained.

The situation is different when we are dealing with individuals or groups viewed as outsiders. When the other people are not members of one's family, financial considerations are likely to become much more significant in evaluating the desirability and value of interactions. If financial gains can be achieved by working with other people or by selecting them for employment, the relationship is likely to occur. On the other hand, if one can make money by *not* working with the others or by *not* selecting them for employment, the relationship does not take place.

These considerations appear to describe the manner in which corporate America interacts with Jews when financial criteria can be clearly identified. If financial considerations explicitly dictate that recruitment and selection of Jews should take place, such activity is more likely to occur. However, if the same criteria suggest that Jews should be neither recruited nor selected, we may expect to see a lessening of such activity. In brief, these are the classic patterns we would expect to see in the treatment of an outsider group by an insider majority that is in control of economic resources and the conditions of employment.

The Arab Boycott of Israel and Its Implications for Employment of American Jews

> There was absolutely no question about it. The Arab nations would not deal with any Jewish executives under any conditions and if we, an American company, expected to do business with them, we were not to send any Jews."

The words are those of a non-Jewish college professor who has been active as a management consultant for many years; he was recounting his years as a full-time employee in the oil industry. The situation he describes is not surprising, and it is consistent with the experience of another interviewee, currently a full-time consultant, who is Jewish. During the years he was employed by a major oil company in a staff position, it was continually made clear to him that any upward executive aspirations on his part were impossible. It was also made clear that any interactions that were taking place between any of the company's Jewish employees/consultants and Arab clients were on a sub-rosa basis and were not to be made public.

These comments are consistent with the data we presented earlier, which indicated that the lowest proportion of Jewish senior managers of the industries examined is in the petroleum industry. Furthermore, as will be shown in a later chapter, it is this same industry that has taken an active interest in developing and instituting affirmative action programs for other minorities besides Jews while continuing to be nonsupportive toward the Jewish employees it does have (*Rights,* 1978).

This pattern is not unique to the oil companies, however; it can also be found in other organizations that have financial relationships with the Arab nations that are supporting an economic boycott against the State of Israel. Companies in various industries in our private sector, American universities, and even the federal government have shown this pattern when economic factors have been involved:

> The activities of the offending companies were sometimes startling in their crudity. Such blunt strictures against employment of Jews had not been heard in decades and had long been outlawed. But here was a teacher recruitment agency issuing job orders for Middle East schools, announcing that teachers who are Jewish, have Jewish surnames, or Jewish ancestors need not apply.
> —A mortgage company offering investments to a Midwest bank provided "no board member or director shall be Jewish."
> —An engineering firm, recruiting for projects under the supervision of the U.S. Army Corps of Engineers, asking applicants to state their religion. . . .
> —A Midwest American medical supplies company which agreed to prohibit Jews from handling any aspect of the shipment of goods under a $20,000,000 contract with Saudi Arabia.
> —An East Coast architectural planning company which told a qualified Jewish applicant he couldn't be hired because it was actively seeking contracts with three Arab countries and had received a letter stipulating that no Jews be employed on the project; another which asked the sales representative of a nationally known building supply firm whether he or his company was Jewish "because we have a contract with Saudi Arabia and it's been implied that we're not to do business with Jews"; a third which eliminated all identifiably Jewish names from its company brochures as part of a sales campaign to solicit Arab business; and yet a fourth working on Saudi Arabian projects under the supervision of the U.S. Army Corps of Engineers, which told Jewish applicants it could not hire them because the contracts prohibited Jewish employees and even the products of certain manufacturers. (Belth, 1981, pp. 243–44)

In addition:

> The worst offender has been the U.S. Army Corps of Engineers which since 1964 has been constructing over $24 billion worth of civilian and military facilities in Saudi Arabia. . . . In 1975 a congressional investigation revealed that the original 1964 agree-

ment with the Saudis stipulated that the Saudis would have the right to veto any American contractors recommended by the Corps—obviously, a clause giving the Saudis the right to bar Jewish firms or firms that employed Jews. But it turned out that the problem was much worse than that. Corps officials admitted that they not only cooperated with the Saudi exclusion policy against Jews, but the Corps itself had decided (without prompting by the Saudi government) to bar any Jewish soldiers and all Jewish employees of American companies from going to Saudi Arabia to work. (Volkman, 1982, p. 277)

These patterns are from a decade ago, but there is continuing evidence that similar incidents continue to take place up to the present day. Of considerable interest, also, is that they continue to occur even when it is not clear that the Arab nations involved have made any explicit discriminatory demands. In 1984, a federal judge awarded two Jewish faculty members of the Baylor University College of Medicine $394,514 because of discrimination resulting from an agreement between that institution and King Faisal Hospital in Saudi Arabia under which the school was to send cardiovascular surgical teams to the Saudi hospital on a rotating basis for three-month shifts, with the Saudis paying the salaries of the visiting doctors. Baylor admitted that it did not assign the plaintiffs—Dr. Laurence M. Abrams and Dr. Stuart A. Linde, both qualified anesthesiologists—because they were Jewish and the school assumed that the Saudis would not grant visas to Jews, even though the Saudis had never told officials at Baylor not to assign Jewish doctors to the project nor did the contract call for such exclusion. One might argue that such anticipatory exclusionist decisions on the part of the Baylor University authorities stemmed from the view that such activity was somehow more permissible against Jews as outsiders in American life than it might have been against some other group.

Other evidence that such discriminatory acts are neither necessary nor above legal recourse is a recent case involving a Jewish engineer who had applied for employment with a company doing work in Saudi Arabia:

A Jewish engineer who charged the Ralph M. Parsons Co., a California-based contracting firm, with religious discrimination for turning him down for a job in Saudi Arabia has received a $72,500 settlement from the company.

The complainant, Morris Hochberg, claimed in his federal suit that although his professional qualifications were never questioned, he was rejected after a Parsons official asked him if he was Jewish and he answered in the affirmative. Hochberg was supported in his suit by the American Jewish Congress. . . .

He filed a complaint with the Equal Employment Opportunities Commission and won the commission's permission to bring suit in a district court in California. His action charged the Parsons Company with violating Title VII of the Civil Rights Act, which prohibits discrimination on grounds of race or religion. The company agreed to pay $72,500 in damages as part of an out-of-court settlement. Without admitting guilt—a customary practice in such agreements—the company promised it would adhere in the future to a policy of processing all applications and applicants for employment with Saudi Arabian employers "in a nondiscriminatory manner, without regard to the religion of any applicant." Parsons also declared that, in the future, it will enforce a company prohibition against any inquiry concerning an applicant's religion. AJ Congress general counsel Will Maslow said this was the second case in which AJ Congress had assisted Jews who had been discriminated against on the basis of religion by American firms doing business with Saudi Arabia. The previous case involved the Trainex Corp. which also agreed to modify its hiring practices after discrimination charges were leveled against it. (*Jewish Week,* 1986, p. 7)

Of major interest is whether such activity on the part of American companies would be countenanced if the applicants were members of groups considered to be insiders in American society. We have no way of knowing at this point what the implications might be and at what point the possibilities of economic gain begin to interact with family considerations in influencing decision making for different types of groups under different conditions. Certainly, there are people who sell their children into slavery, and there are cultures that have encouraged or at least have not punished the murderers of newborn females because of economic factors. Closer to home—and also indicating that money can sometimes override almost all feelings of family/insider status—is the case of Lessing Rosenwald, a major Jewish stockholder in Sears Roebuck who acquiesced in the anti-Semitism of the Sears chief executive on the grounds that the company was showing high profits under his leadership (Birmingham, 1984). Clearly, we cannot assume that the relationship between economic motivation and insider-outsider status is a perfect one. However, the relationship is there, particularly in the case of Americans who happen to be Jews and who become involved in the activities of companies that deal in economic relationships with the Arab world.

When Financial Criteria Dictate Selection: Some Changes in Commercial Banking?

The relationship we are proposing is strengthened by evidence that Jews are more likely to be considered for employment when specific economic benefits can be perceived, regardless of the history of the organizations or industries involved. One industry in which this may be beginning to occur is commercial banking—an industry that, as we have seen, has rarely had much of a Jewish presence.

Perhaps the major stimulus underlying the possibility of change in this industry has been the general climate of deregulation in many Western economies in recent years, which has led to great competition for commercial banking from other financial institutions. Such competition has had a major impact on an industry that has traditionally relied on personal contact and insider group collegiality as a basis for business growth and development. Social acceptability in business relationships and in personal relationships was always the foundation upon which commercial bankers were able to develop and maintain their institutions. This perceived need for social acceptability, for reasons we have already given, traditionally underlay the lack of interest in employing Jews in executive roles.

However, with the growth in the 1970s of worldwide corporations and financial markets, innovative methods of financing corporate operations, and the possibilities of new sources of financial gain, the view that successful commercial banking must be based on social acceptability began to come under some question. Corporations that for years had typically gone to their commercial bankers for financing found themselves challenged by competitors that financed their operations at lower rates and had developed new sources of profit. Such competitive pressures increasingly forced some of the traditional clients of the commercial banks to seek out financial channels where they could get the highest interest rates for their funds and where they could finance their borrowing needs at the lowest possible cost. Another significant influence on these trends was the boom in the merger-acquisition activities of major corporations that began to take place in the 1980s and the various going-private, going-public strategies followed by different companies (and sometimes by the same company at different times). Suddenly, new methods of financing operations became household words in a world increasingly fascinated by the various corporate strategies. The commercial banking organizations began to feel increasing pressure from their stockholders and employees to do something to remain competitive.

The result of all this has been a change in the marketing and sales strategies of many commercial banks as they attempt to meet aggressively the competition from these other types of financing institutions and as they try to compete successfully in a world where the demand for social acceptability may be becoming less significant. According to some reports, one way in which this pressure has begun to manifest itself has been an increase in the willingness of commercial banks to hire members of ethnic groups previously not viewed favorably for significant positions—for example, Jewish and Italian Americans (Bennett, 1986). There is some anecdotal evidence that in recent years, such famous New York—based commercial banks as Citibank, Chemical and Manufacturers Hanover have begun to hire a number of individuals from these groups with backgrounds in such aggressive, new areas of major commercial banking interest as consumer banking and loans to small and medium sized firms. It should also be noted, however, that the actual number of individuals involved in these so-called trendbreakers is quite small and that, in a few of the cases cited, the Jews who have been hired by the commercial banks are in the more traditional (less organizational powerfully) areas of Jewish opportunity, such as staff and professional positions, rather than line management.

There is also other evidence that supports economic motivation as a possible justification for selecting Jews for employment in a particular context. There are the practices, cited earlier, of life insurance companies, which were more likely to hire Jews for sales and sales-related positions in communities and cities with large percentages of Jews but less likely to hire Jews for offices in areas where there were few Jewish residents. Also, both the Ohio State and Michigan studies of anti-Semitism in work organizations found that fear of customer reaction was one of the major factors affecting a company's willingness to select Jews for employment or the degree to which they were considered promotable to executive positions.

9
Organizational Characteristics and Hostility toward Outsiders

There has long been research support for the proposition that organizations that differ in terms of structural and process variables will also systematically differ in terms of behavioral and attitudinal characteristics (Smircich, 1983). Among the organizational dimensions that have been examined within this context are the degree of hierarchical structure, task specialization, and role routinization. There is reason to believe that high levels of each of these organizational characteristics may negatively affect the degree to which Jews may be given the opportunity for managerial and/or executive positions. One reason why this relationship may occur is that such organizations are less willing to employ or accept in other ways those who are outsiders or those who are different from the mainstream because of the attitudes and norms encouraged by these organizations. Since Jews are considered outsiders, we would therefore expect that such organizations would be more likely to be hostile toward Jews and not to employ them (as well as other outsiders) than organizations that cannot be characterized in this manner. A second possible explanation for this relationship, not necessarily antithetical to the first, rests on two factors. First, hierarchical leaders and authority figures can generally get their subordinates to do whatever they desire, including being aggressive and hostile toward others regardless of who these others might be. Second, as Kipnis (1976) has shown, there is evidence that the sense of power over others that comes with hierarchical control appears to encourage aggression and hostility against those who are lower in the status hierarchy. The combined effect of these factors tends to increase any latent hostility or aggressiveness that may already exist in the organization, including the aggression that may already exist against outsider groups. As a result, organizations that have strong hierarchies tend to be more aggressive in general and particularly more aggressive against the traditional objects of aggression—outsiders.

The Effect of Hierarchical Status and Authority on Hostility toward Others

The hypothesis that hierarchical status and authority relative to others directly influences and facilitates hostility toward others has received extensive support in the research studies of Kipnis (1976) and Milgram (1974). The former has found consistently that those with hierarchical power over others, regardless of the characteristics of the individuals involved, will consistently engage in acts designed to deprecate those who are lower in the hierarchy. Having hierarchical power apparently generates the motivation to deprecate others. It also gives the power-holding individual the ability to convince those who report to him or her to deprecate others, regardless of the motivational antecedents of such desires.

One of the more famous psychological experiments showing how authority figures can directly influence us to do violence to others is Milgram's (1974) research, which demonstrated that people from all walks of life would, at the behest of authority figures such as those posing as research scientists, administer what they believed to be electric shocks to others, despite the protests and apparent great discomfort of the "victims." Although these experiments did not really provide any new information to those who are familiar with the history of humans' brutality to humans, they did illustrate graphically how those with authority may influence so-called normal people to engage in hostile behavior toward others for little apparent justification or cause except the behest of the authority figure. To some psychologists, such demonstrations provide at least one form of psychological explanation for the brutalities often engaged in the name of religious, racial, and other forms of discrimination.

At a less dramatic level, we see similar processes operating in the research by Quinn et al. (1968), discussed earlier. Among their findings was a consistent pattern indicating that discrimination against Jews was a function of the perceived lack of concern for such acts by the authority figures in the organization. When the managers believed that their company cared significantly about the principle of equal employment opportunity, only 17 percent were likely to discriminate against Jews. The comparable figure for the same question was 46 percent for managers who believed that their company did not really care about equal employment opportunity but, at least partially, paid only lip service to it. Quinn and his co-workers also found that the effect of authority figures who did "not care" about discrimination was stronger when there was a preexisting willingness to discriminate among the managers. Of the managers who were intensely against Jews to begin with, 68 percent were likely to discriminate against Jews if they felt that their company did not care much about discrimination, as opposed to 29 percent of the managers who also were intensely against Jews but thought their company would be strongly opposed to discriminatory action. Similarly, the figures on readiness to discriminate were 24 percent for those who did not have intense anti-Semitic feelings and thought their company did not care and 8 percent for those who did not have such feelings against Jews but thought their company did care about equal employment opportunity practices.

The evidence for the impact of direct hierarchical social influence on hostile acts toward others, regardless of who they might be, is not difficult to demonstrate. It is there and it must be considered in any examination of the effect of organizational characteristics on the relationship between Jews and corporate America, for its impact is to increase aggression and hostility in general against all groups.

Hierarchical Organizations and Intolerance
of Outsiders, Variations, and Differences

A lack of tolerance for "differences" and for those who are deviant from the norm is more likely to be found in hierarchical organizations that stress routine and specialization because individuals tend to develop attitudinal and cognitive structures that reflect their job experience (Breer and Locke, 1965). Those whose experience is in organizational structures that stress everyday sameness, routine, and job specialization without variety will learn and internalize a lack of tolerance of difference and unpredictability because of the nature of their experience and because the organizations they work for encourage predictability and lack of variation from expected norms. In such organizations, predictability and routine become very important at all levels, and allowing variation from the comfort of familiarity by selecting "outsiders" for responsible managerial and executive positions becomes a source of anxiety. The deviation is important emotionally and it may also be important financially (or at least perceived as such), in that such hiring practices might generate extra costs and problems because of the (believed) lack of predictability of the so-called deviant individual. Supporting these tendencies even further is that the lack of tolerance for variation in such organizations will lead to the development and reinforcement of cultural values that support hostility toward outsiders, since such cultural values would support the behavioral actions. The structural and the cultural factors are thus mutually supportive and strengthen one another. In this interactive, mutually reinforcing manner, the structural characteristics, the cultural norms, and the individual attitudes would make it increasingly likely over time that organizations marked by strong hierarchies, high specialization, and high routinization would allow and encourage hostile actions toward outsiders. It is in such organizations that we are more likely to find actions and policies directed against Jews and other outsiders, either overtly or in a habitual, nonthinking, noncaring manner. The hierarchical, routinized organization and the sameness of everyday life that it calls for provide the mechanism by which intolerance of variability and outsiders is developed, and the insider-outsider factor and the view of Jews (and others) as outsiders marks them as permissible targets for such intolerance.

Some research studies have been generally supportive of these proposals, but the evidence they cite has unfortunately not always been directly relevant to the world of work and jobs and the relationship between Jews and American corporations. One problem is that few of these studies focus on attitudes and behavior toward Jews as a specific group in a work setting. Typically, the research has dealt with outsiders as a general category or with groups other than Jews; if they have dealt with Jews at all, it has been Jews as part of an outsider group. A second problem is that many of the studies have taken place in non-work settings.

Yet even with these shortcomings, the findings of these investigations are generally consistent with the arguments made here. My review of the impact of work experience on civil-libertarian attitudes several years ago is particularly relevant in this context:

> Work experience marked by hierarchical approaches to leadership, specialization of duties, and routinization of tasks tends to be associated with attitudes and behaviors that can be described as non-civil libertarian in nature—i.e., low toleration of differences, hostility to variation, and aggression towards others because they are different. . . . while the general relationship seems fairly well-established, there are cases where it does not hold (Levison, 1974).
>
> A well-known study which illustrates this relationship is Kornhauser's (1965) research on the mental health of the automobile worker. . . . What is of most relevance here is the finding that the more the job involved routinization, specialization, and acceptance of hierarchical control, the more the individual exhibited hostility towards others, had relatively traditional conservative attitudes toward racial integration. . . . In a similar vein, McWhinney (cited in Jenkins, 1973) has reported that workers in a plant where hierarchy, specialization, and routinization had been deemphasized became more active in overcoming civil rights and civil libertarian problems in their communities.
>
> Additional support . . . may be found in Greenhaus, Korman and Gavin (1974). . . . In this research . . . perceptions of organi-

zational climate were obtained for 258 managers at different levels . . . and related to expressed willingness to accept minority-group members and women as managers within the organization. In all cases those dimensions directly relevant to the proposition (authoritarian control, bureaucratic control, and openness of communication) were as predicted. (Korman, 1975, pp. 139–40)

The general argument that hierarchical structure decreases tolerance for and minimizes acceptance of different groups and people is supported by other investigations besides those already cited. The following are among the findings of these other studies:

1. Programming, hierarchy, and routinization in organizations is negatively related to acceptance of variation (Guetzkow, 1965).

2. Membership in occupations with specialized characteristics has been shown to be negatively related to a liking for and acceptability of occupations with different characteristics (Korman, 1963).

3. Employment in a pyramid-shaped organization is negatively related to performance on tasks calling for receptivity to change and variation (Maier and Hoffman, 1961).

4. Exposure to sensitivity-training groups that emphasize non-hierarchy and nonspecialization of activities decreases prejudice toward others (Rubin, 1967).

5. Hostility between labor and management groups can be decreased by incorporating both into a larger group that emphasizes nonhierarchy, nonspecialization of activities, non-programming, and where equal status is stressed (Blake, Mouton, and Sloma, 1965; Blake and Mouton, 1966).

6. Rotating individuals from group to group in nonspecialized roles decreases the degree of conflict among them (Deutsch, 1969).

7. The more homogenous and specialized a work group is and the more physically separated it is from others, the more

likely it is that the group will engage in strikes and other hostile activities (Kerr and Siegel, 1954).

The hypothesis that hierarchical status and role specialization negatively affect tolerance for others has received additional support in the years since these findings were reported, but again, unfortunately, not in the areas of direct concern here. Typical of such work have been the research findings on the "contact hypothesis" (Amir, 1969). This hypothesis has generated remarkably consistent findings over the years (Stephan and Brigham, 1985), supporting the proposition that contact between two groups results in increased liking between the groups *if* the contact has been between two groups of equal status. However, the contact does not result in increased liking if the contact has been between two groups of different hierarchical status.

Also supporting the general logic underlying the contact hypothesis is that individuals who are socialized in family and other social settings marked by strong hierarchical control tend to be more generally prejudicial toward outsiders such as minority group members in American society (for example, Jews) than those who are socialized in families marked by egalitarianism and the absence of strong stress on rules and procedures. These conclusions—originally proposed in *The Authoritarian Personality* (Adorno et al., 1950), based on research at the University of California at Berkeley—were important in themselves and were also used as a base for generating the famous *F*-scale, a measure shown in much later research to be highly related to prejudicial attitudes toward a variety of outsider groups and individuals, such as the blind, the deaf, and various ethnic groups (Korman, 1971b). Most relevant for us here is that individuals with high scores on this scale—that is, those who were most prejudiced and distant from those who were "different"—are more likely to have been reared in families with high degrees of hierarchical control and rule orientation. It is important that we keep in mind, however, that little of this research, interesting as it is, has taken place in work settings. As a result, we have little indication of the degree to which personality factors such as those measured by the *F*-scale actually influence inequitable behavior toward Jews and other outsiders in the work setting.

In fact, the problem with the *F*-scale research is illustrative of one of the two major problems with many of the findings cited in this chapter concerning the influence of hierarchy on the specific choice of Jews as target. The problem is that much of this research, particularly that stemming from the contact hypothesis, has taken place in laboratory settings, in school desegregation field studies, and in other non-employment-related group settings. This lack of research in the actual work context is important because the setting of the work organization is different from that of schools and college laboratory experiments. A real-world work organization has a culture and a history, and these have an impact on the nature of the processes involved. Thus, although the findings are reasonably consistent regarding the impact of hierarchical characteristics and rule emphasis on the likelihood of choosing outsiders as targets for discriminatory acts, so little of the research has taken place in work settings that we must conclude, at least at this time, that this is, at best, only a hypothesis worth considering.

A second problem is that few studies—in or out of the work setting—have utilized behavior and attitudes toward Jews specifically. Although attitudes and behaviors toward Jews in corporate America may share some components with attitudes and behaviors toward all groups viewed as outsiders or as different from the mainstream of American life, there may also be some unique aspects of all these groups that need to be kept in mind. Jewish Americans are not Black Americans nor Hispanic Americans nor Asian Americans. Each of these groups is different—economically, educationally, historically, culturally, and behaviorally. Although they have problems in common, they also have problems that are unique to each. This suggests that research relating to each group should be undertaken separately, at least on some occasions if we wish to understand fully the relationship between each group and corporate America.

10
Reactions to Equal Opportunity Programs: The Internalization of Outsider Status

P rograms designed to increase minority group representation in the professions and other types of employment fall essentially into two categories. One type of program seeks to encourage, morally and financially, efforts by corporate America and other employers and training institutions to seek out, recruit, and employ members of specified minority groups. Also characteristic of such programs—but less likely to be mentioned, at least publicly—is that these efforts are not encouraged for other groups. Programs of this nature are sometimes instituted under court order, but often there has been no legal stimulus.

A second type of program results from court orders for explicit types of hiring procedures. Typical of such orders were those enunciated in the Supreme Court ruling on July 2, 1986, which legalized reverse discrimination in personnel decision making against white (non-Jewish and Jewish) males in the United States under certain conditions:

> The Supreme Court today firmly endorsed the use of affirmative action in the workplace to cure past discrimination against minority groups when less dramatic approaches would not work. The Court did so in two cases in which it ruled that, as a remedy for job discrimination, judges may sometimes order racial preferences that benefit minority groups who are not personally victims of discrimination.

Six of the Court's nine members explicitly rejected the Reagan Administration's argument that judges have not the power to order job preferences for minority group members at the expense of white employees unless all who benefit have personally suffered from discrimination. (Taylor, 1986, pp. A1, B9)

In examining these programs—both differential recruiting efforts and legalized forms of reverse discrimination—it is important to realize that the two types of efforts would be expected to have similar impact, since they are based on a similar rationale, regardless of their origins or legal standing—that is, the substitution of group membership for individual ability as a basis for selection and other personnel actions. As a result of such substitution, individuals who are not in the favored or desired groups are less likely to be recruited, to be selected, and to be favorably evaluated for any other type of personnel decision *simply on the basis of group membership alone.* The results and the processes would be similar whether the specific, concrete actions in a particular case involved corporate recruiting, specific recruitment advertising attempts, tag lines in general announcements indicating that special consideration will be given to members of specific groups, or the development of collaborative recruitment efforts with advocate groups seeking to increase the representation of their membership in a particular labor force. All such efforts can be expected to work to the advantage of those who are members of these special groups and to the disadvantage of those who are not.

It is clear that these programs, now legally sanctioned by the U.S. Supreme Court, call for discriminatory decision making on at least three counts. First, they call for the recruitment and employment of members of a particular group on the basis of group membership, regardless of the implications for the employment of those who do not belong to that group. Second, they call for discriminatory actions regardless of whether or not the majority group members who will be negatively affected by the employment decisions have ever personally discriminated against minorities. Third, discriminatory actions are now allowable regardless of the scores of job applicants on instruments and measures normally used for selection procedures. In this last instance, the Court ruled in *Johnson v. Santa Clara County Transportation Agency* that a woman should be given hiring preference over a man, even though she scored slightly lower on a test used for selection for that position, in order to increase what the Court perceived to be a gross under-representation of women in the particular job category. The implications are clear, on the basis of the *Johnson* case, regarding the types of administrative efforts that may be used to achieve these differential recruitment goals. Discrimination in recruitment and selection on the basis of group membership has been legalized by the U.S. Supreme Court.

The problems involved in these issues are immense and there should be no doubt about their significance. On the one hand, virtually all observers would agree that we, as a society, have too frequently tolerated racial, sexual, religious, and other forms of bias in employment decisions. Similarly, almost everyone in American society wants to see such biased decision making eliminated once and for all. On the other hand, we now see increasingly, in the interest of eliminating this previous bias, differential recruitment and hiring procedures that use group membership rather than ability as a basis for selection. It is paradoxical, to say the least, for a culture that has always prided itself (sometimes unrealistically) on using ability and performance as a basis for favorable evaluation to use such discriminatory decision making and then justify it on the basis it is the way to eliminate discrimination in employment decision making.

The situation has not been made any easier by the highly controversial Supreme Court decisions in this area. Originally, in the cases presented to the court regarding selection and promotion decisions, the Court concluded that reverse discrimination was justified if it was clear that there was evidence of a long-standing bias against members of certain minority groups and that that bias had been resistant to any prior efforts at change. However, in the *Johnson* case, this constraint was eliminated, and reverse discrimination is now allowed as a basis for employment decision making, even when there is no history of discrimination, so long as the job does not require specific training. Group membership has now been legally sanctioned by the Supreme Court as a basis for both recruitment and selection in a wide variey of situations whose limits, if any, are still not defined. In brief, the Supreme Court has legalized bias in employment decision making under certain apparently expanding conditions. Though applauded by some groups, these decisions for discrimination in favor of certain defined minority groups have been bitterly attacked by others as the legalization of reverse discrimination. According to this latter group of constitutional scholars, decisions of this nature violate our traditions and our laws and unfairly injure the work and career opportunities of any individuals who seek to be evaluated on the basis of job capability rather than group membership. To quote the late Professor Alexander Bickel of Yale University:

> "The lessons of the great decisions of the Supreme Court and the lessons of contemporary history have been the same for at least a generation: discrimination on the basis of race is illegal, immoral, unconstitutional, inherently wrong and destructive of democratic society. Now this is to be unlearned and we are told that this is not a matter of fundamental principle but only a matter of whose ox is gored. Those for whom racial equality was demanded are to be more equal than others. Having found support in the Constitution for equality, they now claim support for inequality under the same Constitution." (Belth, 1981, p. 203).

Similarly, there is the written opinion of Supreme Court Justice Scalia in his dissent to the *Johnson* decision:

> In a blistering dissent, Justice Antonin Scalia said the Court's "enormous expansion" of prior decisions upholding affirmative action had completed its conversion of a 1964 antidiscrimination law into an "engine of discrimination" against men and whites, especially the "unknown, unaffluent, unorganized." (Taylor, 1987, p. A1)

Supreme Court Decisions, Equal Opportunity and Affirmative Action Programs, and Jewish Employment

These Supreme Court decisions and these employment trends have posed serious questions for concerned individuals in the Jewish

American community. Given the commitment among most Jews to the civil rights movement—both for themselves and for others—difficulties have developed on a number of fronts. One problem stems from the historical reality that Jews have done well in the United States as a group because of the greater commitment by this country to the principle of individual differences in ability and motivation as a basis for occupational advancement and to the principle of a free market (imperfect though it has been) in employment opportunities. Now Jews in the United States are suddenly faced with a reimposition of government-sanctioned utilization of group categories as a basis for employment-related recruitment and selection. Such programs are a problem for Jews because of their historical meaning and because there is now an issue of legitimate self-interest—since Jews, particularly Jewish males, are among the groups against whom discrimination has been sanctioned. The problem is not much better for Jewish women, even though they are officially included in the minority group categories. However, because they are included in these programs and under these legal guidelines as women, not as Jews, their likelihood of attaining a job under these procedures is a function of their percentage of the total number of women involved in a given situation rather than their abilities and their competence. This could mean that Jewish women might be limited to 2.5 percent of the placements in a particular job, rather than being able to compete in an open market for however many positions their ability and competence have prepared them for. For both groups, Jewish men and Jewish women, decisions such as that in the *Johnson* case have meant that the significance of the ability to perform a job as a basis for hiring has been decreased in favor of a group membership criterion. This situation could easily lead to a decline in job/career possibilities for Jewish males and, to a slightly lesser degree, for Jewish women (since Jewish women are so few in number relative to the number of women in the labor force).

The foregoing argument is also relevant if the implications of an even more recent Supreme Court decision are considered from the viewpoint of their effects on affirmative-action programs. In parallel cases involving the defacing of a synagogue in suburban Maryland (*Shaare Tefila Congregation v. Cobb*) and the denial of academic tenure to a professor of Arab ancestry by a college in Pennsylvania (*St. Francis College v. Al Khazraji*), the Supreme Court ruled on May 18, 1987, that the Civil Rights Act of 1866 permitted federal lawsuits claiming intentional discrimination against a person because of ethnic characteristics. According to the decision, such suits were permissible on the basis of any major ethnic characteristics, such as Jewish religious faith or Arab ancestry.

Since this decision appears to contradict the decision in *Johnson v. Santa Clara County,* there is currently considerable confusion regarding the actual degree of discrimination permitted for affirmative action purposes and the conditions under which such actions may take place. In this sense, a legal limbo has developed that will have to be clarified by future Supreme Court decisions; these decisions are difficult to predict considering the inconsistent pattern that we have just described. Regardless of any future decisions, however, it should be made clear that even if Jews were to be included in any future affirmative action categories, the effects will be negative for Jews (because of their minimal percentage in the population) and, more important, for American society in general if by such actions we move even further from the use of individual ability to the use of non-competence-based group membership as the basis for recruitment and selection decisions. Whether discrimination results from informal insider-outsider factors or from legal support systems, its impact is the same. It hurts the ability of a society to survive and it hurts any minority group, Jewish or otherwise, for whom the most equitable criterion for advancement has been the ability to perform the job or task in question. For these reasons, it is essentially irrelevant whether or not Jews are eventually granted "favored group" treatment.

These are the theoretical implications of preferential-group hiring programs for Jewish employment that are based on logical and numerical considerations. There is also empirical evidence demonstrating the negative impact of these programs on Jews, although it is difficult to determine that impact. One problem is that it is difficult to determine the number of individuals, Jewish and non-Jewish, who have actually been victims of explicit discriminatory decisions as a result of such programs. Employers are understandably reluctant even to gather such data, much less publicize it.

Another problem is that it is difficult to know how the processes of self-selection have operated in cases where affirmative action has been anticipated. How many Jewish applicants and others have not even bothered to apply for a particular position (or professional school) if there is a belief that an employer is looking for members of a particular minority group? It is hard even to make estimates in these contexts. Another source of difficulty is that an accurate estimate of the effects of these programs would require a knowledge of the number of non-minority-group members who might have been hired in an open employment market when the only criterion was predicted ability to perform a particular job. Such a figure would then have to be compared to the number of non-minority-group members hired when at least part of the employer's recruitment effort has been specifically aimed at a limited number of groups—ignoring other potential job applicants. These are only some of the problems in developing a fair assessment of the actual and potential impact of these programs. Yet despite such problems, there is evidence that these programs have had a negative impact on Jewish employment in the past and may do so even more in the future.

A Case Study of the Effects of Affirmative Action Programs: The Oil Industry

One study that demonstrates the negative implications of affirmative action programs is the investigation by the Anti-Defamation League (*Rights,* 1978) of employment patterns related to Jews and other minorities in what were then the top six American oil firms. The following were among the major findings reported in this study:

1. Oil company discrimination against Jews was found to take several forms: (a) classic discrimination patterns, such as lack of recruitment, limitations on promotion, nonassignment to certain job areas, and stereotyped job assignments; (b) insensitivity to religious observance requirements; (c)

maintenance of corporate membership in restrictive clubs; and (d) discrimination as a result of the Arab boycott.

2. Of the 300 top job holders in the industry, only 5 were Jews.

3. There was not a single instance of recruitment advertising by any oil company in any English-language Jewish newspaper.

4. A study of Jewish referral sources revealed only one case of an oil company attempt at recruitment. This pattern is highly consistent with the report by Slavin and Pradt (1982), who found that seven of the major oil (or related) companies made no visits at all to colleges with 30 percent or more Jewish students, whereas they made from fourteen to forty-eight recruiting attempts at schools with fewer than 30 percent Jewish undergraduates.

5. Interviews with Jewish employees of oil companies revealed little hope for promotion (while company recruitment activities were stressing advancement possibilities for other minorities and for women).

6. As shown in table 10–1, virtually all of the oil companies showed significant increases in employment of women and other minorities during the previous decade, but no such pattern was discernible for Jews.

Yet despite the discrepant patterns in employment and recruitment activities between Jews and other minority groups found by the ADL researchers, and despite the increases in employment for these other minorities, the report also states that oil industry representatives continued to insist that religious discrimination is of minor importance in the industry. The report suggests that one possible reason for such claims and the refusal to confront the data presented was the continuing failure by the federal government to enforce 41CFR60—the federal regulation that forbids religious discrimination among federal contractors (which includes virtually all oil companies)—a failure admitted to by the head of the Office of Federal Contract Compliance.

Table 10–1

Effects of Affirmative Action Programs on Levels of Minority Group Employment in Oil Industry Firms

Company	Year	Percentage of Employees				
		Female	Spanish Surname	Black	Oriental	American Indian
Exxon	1973	12.38		2.96		
	1976	15.31		4.09		
Texaco	1966	9.99	1.79	3.30	0.20	.03
	1976	11.37	3.42	7.24	0.49	.31
Standard Oil of California	1966	9.10				
	1975	14.00				
Gulf	1971	16.08		5.36		
	1977	18.60		10.20		
Shell	1966	15.60				
	1976	19.00				

Source: "A Study of Jewish Employment Problems in the Big Six Oil Company Headquarters," *Rights* 9 (1978), pp. 22, 27, 30, 32, 35.

The Demonstrated and Potential Impact of Affirmative Action Programs on Jewish Employment

There is evidence relating to the impact of affirmative action programs on Jewish employment in a number of legal suits. In perhaps the most significant of these cases, a federal grand jury in Brooklyn, New York, awarded $275,000 to David Krulik, an employee of the New York City Board of Education, who claimed to have been discriminated against because he was Jewish (Lipman, 1984). At one time, Krulik had been the highest-ranking official in the city's "English as a Second Language" program, and he had authored a number of books in the area. However, despite his background and years of experience, the reorganization by the NYC Board of Education of the Office of Bilingual Education under a black Hispanic woman had left Krulik without any duties or responsibilities. At the same time, seven other individuals, none of whom was Jewish, were appointed to higher ranks and levels of authority. After continual requests for job assignments were turned down, Krulik finally sued the NYC Board of Education on the basis that the acts of the supervisor constituted "reverse discrimination." The suit—the first ever brought against the NYC Board of Education by a Jewish plaintiff—was upheld in federal court, thus establishing a precedent for the future (assuming that later appeals of the case are decided the same way).

Of considerable importance, in addition to demonstrated impact, is the question of the *potential* significance of affirmative action programs. How many Jews might conceivably be affected by these programs in the future, if they have not already been so affected? Recently gathered data suggest that the numbers of Jews who may feel such impact may be considerable, both in professional school admission practices and in actual job settings. Like most Americans, most Jews, professional and otherwise, are organizational employees, subject to all the constraints and pressures involved in such status and particularly to the negative implications for their employment that stem from such decisions as *Johnson v. Santa Clara County Transportation Agency*. Besides such potential impact on employed Jews at all economic levels, it has been estimated that approximately 15 percent of the Jewish population have incomes at or below the poverty level (Rosenblatt, 1985). This figure is consistent with an independent survey of the Jewish population of Los Angeles, which found that approximately 40 percent were at the economically marginal level, with annual total family incomes of $15,000 or less, and that about half of those (about 20 percent of the Jewish population of Los Angeles) were below the poverty level (Waxman, 1983). These figures are also consistent with those gathered for the city of New York in 1981, which are shown in table 10–2. As indicated in the table, approximately one in five Jewish families in both Brooklyn and the Bronx had incomes below $10,000 a year, while 35 to 40 percent of the Jewish families in those boroughs were below the marginal household income level of $20,000 per year. Even taking the entire New York metropolitan area as a whole, including the affluent suburbs, there are more Jewish families with household incomes below $20,000 a year (27 percent) than above $50,000 a year (20 percent).

For individuals at any level of employment—but particularly

Table 10–2

Household Incomes as Percentages of Total, New York
Metropolitan Area Jewish Population, 1981

County of Residence	Incomes ($000)						
	< 10	*10–19*	*20–29*	*30–39*	*40–49*	*50–59*	*>60*
Bronx	18	17	32	16	10	3	4
Brooklyn	20	28	20	15	14	2	1
Manhattan	9	15	18	15	17	4	22
Queens	13	14	24	21	17	5	6
Richmond	7	16	20	26	26	3	2
Nassau	4	4	14	15	19	17	27
Suffolk	5	13	19	20	21	8	14
Westchester	3	11	13	11	17	11	34
Total	11	16	20	17	16	6	14

Source: Paul Ritterband and Steven M. Cohen, "The Social Characteristics of the New York Area Jewish Community, 1981," in M. Himmelfarb and D. Singer (eds.), *American Jewish Yearbook, 1984* (New York: American Jewish Committee, 1983).

for those at lower economic levels—any type of job discrimination, under whatever guise it is presented, may be an urgent matter of everyday existence. The ideological wrong of discrimination is bad enough, but the practical impact is even greater for individuals who are attempting to survive with such incomes or, sometimes, with no income at all.

> At least 55,000 New York–area Jews are unemployed, and the number could worsen unless existing training and job-creation programs are strengthened, according to two Queens College studies. . . .
> Herbert Bienstock, director of the Queens College Center for Labor and Urban Programs, Research and Analysis . . . said he found that the majority of unemployed Jews are college graduates and middle-level managers. . . .
> Bienstock also warned that the figures are conservative. They include only persons registered at federal employment centers, not part-time workers, recent college graduates or people who have given up looking for work.
> The total number of Jews either unemployed or underemployed . . . may be as high as 160,000 for the metropolitan area, with 105,000 of them in New York City. . . . There are

approximately 1.68 million Jews living in the region with approximately 1.09 million in the employment pool. (*New York Jewish
Week,* 1987, p. 4).

The Paradoxical Reactions of Jewish Agencies
and Community Leaders

Paradoxically, despite their already demonstrated negative impact
and despite their potential future implications for the employment
and career opportunities of Jews, equal opportunity and affirmative
action programs have generally not been protested by the majority
of Jewish agencies. In fact—perhaps even more paradoxically—
they have been supported by most such groups. The following pas-
sage, which discusses an article by Albert Vorspan of the Union of
American Hebrew Congregations—a major Jewish leader in the
area of civil rights and a leader of the Reform movement of American Jewry—is illustrative of these paradoxical positions:

> The Anti-Defamation League of B'nai B'rith's "tough line" on
> affirmative-action "has been isolated and is now clearly a minority
> position within the Jewish community," according to Albert Vors-
> pan, senior vice-president of the Union of American Hebrew Con-
> gregations (Reform).
>   In a major article on affirmative-action in the Winter, 1986
> issue of *Women's American ORT Reporter,* Vorspan notes that
> "The American Jewish Committee and . . . Congress have contin-
> ued to oppose 'quotas' but both support 'goals' and 'timetables'.
> The AJCongress and Women's American ORT even support quo-
> tas where a court finds a demonstrable pattern of discrimination
> and fixes a quota as a court-ordered remedy." All the national
> Jewish agencies (except for the ADL and Orthodox Union) op-
> pose the Administration's Justice Department stand . . . to nullify
> consent decrees, patiently and carefully achieved in 56 towns and
> counties across the U.S., according to Vorspan. . . . By what co-
> lossal ineptitude could the Jewish community, long-time partner
> to the Black community in the common struggle for a decent soci-

ety, make itself appear as the chief opponent of affirmative action—the very program Blacks see as their last best hope for America? (*Jewish Currents,* 1986, p. 30–31)

There is considerable other evidence supporting Vorspan's claims regarding the predominant attitudes expressed by the leaders of Jewish community agencies. Among those who have publicly proclaimed such support is B'nai B'rith Women, a major group in the spectrum of American Jewish communal organizations (Tomchin, 1985). Support of these programs by leaders of some of the major Jewish organizations is also seen in the outcome of a meeting in December 1984 of a group of black and Jewish civil rights leaders in New York City. At the conclusion of their discussions, they published a list of the most immediate concerns on which they would focus their efforts. The issues listed were primarily relevant to the black community—that is, the anger concerning apartheid in South Africa, the need for more quality in the New York City educational system, and the demand for a more positive stance on affirmative action. Missing were such concerns of the Jewish community as the need to support Israel and the negative implications of affirmative action goals and quotas for Jewish employment. The latter problems were considered less important and were put on the back burner to be dealt with at a later time.

It is fair to conclude that Vorspan's summary of the position of major Jewish agencies in this country relative to affirmative action and other programs that stress favoritism in the recruiting and selection of minority groups besides Jews is accurate. With the exception of the Anti-Defamation League of B'nai B'rith and some groups from the Orthodox spectrum of Jewish life, few Jewish agencies appear to have been willing to recognize or apparently even discuss the negative implications of these programs for Jewish employment, professional or otherwise.

The question we may ask is why: Why the lack of protest? Why the lack of discussion? Why the willingness to ignore and forget the history of Jewish American experience with quotas and limitations on enrollment in professional schools? Why has there been such a reaction to these programs among the majority of Jewish groups?

The Acceptance of Outsider Status
and Its Implications

Two characteristics of the American Jewish community render these reactions understandable. One is that the view of Jews as outsiders in American society also describes and has been accepted by the Jewish community itself. Second, Jews, both individually and collectively—and like other individuals and groups—will often act in a manner that is consistent with such self-accepted status (Korman, 1970). This process, better known as equity motivation, has been studied increasingly in recent years as a key factor underlying the nature of human decision making.

We explore here the significance of these two characteristics more completely to help us better understand the seemingly paradoxical reactions of much of the leadership of the American Jewish community.

Self-Perceptions of Jews as Outsiders in American Life

A key factor in the explanation we are proposing is that Jews, for the most part, agree with the view that they are outsiders in American society. One major reason for the acceptance and internalization of this perception is that Jews are subject to many of the same influences as non-Jews in the placement of Jews, as a group, within an overall cultural context. All individuals must make judgments as to physical and social reality to adapt successfully to their environments. The two types of judgments depend on different types of evidence, however, and are normally made with different degrees of confidence. Physical reality judgments are easier to make and are usually made with more confidence because they are objective and physically based. Since social reality judgments are more difficult to make because of the lack of objective physical evidence, it is usually more necessary to rely on the degree of consensus that one perceives regarding the social object in question. The larger the proportion of individuals in a given setting who claim a certain social reality and the more important such individuals are, the more such views begin to dominate the views of all individuals in that setting, regardless of the original opinions and views involved. The power of majority-based social opinions has been demonstrated time and time again. In fact, such social cues are so powerful that they can sometimes override the influence of physical cues. In one of the most famous experiments in the history of social psychology, Asch (1956) showed how group pressures can sometimes influence people to express judgments that are in violation of clear, unambiguous physical reality.

The acceptance of social reality judgments from a proportionately greater group, even if not always flattering to the self, is therefore firmly based in psychological research. Taken alone, it would seem to account, at least in part, for the internalization by American Jews of their status as outsiders in American life. However, this is not the only factor. There has also been the great influence of history, which points clearly to the fact that, from the viewpoint of survival alone, Jews have had little alternative for two thousand years except to accept such judgments from the dominant groups in any culture in which they were living.

As noted in chapter 1, the separate identity and social patterns that have characterized Jewish life still remain as a social reality of American life, as does the influence of historical cultural patterns. Jews are still outsiders in American life and in corporate America, and they view themselves as such for the most part. It is such self-recognition of their outsider status that has generated, in part, their positive evaluation of careers that take them out from under the control of others—for example, self-controlled occupations such as entrepreneurial and professional careers.

Such self-recognition as outsiders also underlies the continuing alliances of Jews in this country with other outsider groups in American life, despite the fact that these other groups may have a different heritage, a different culture, and different income levels. None of these possibly differentiating influences have appeared to impede significantly the willingness of most Jews in this country to exert their efforts with these others in order to attain civil rights goals believed to be common to all. Despite the strains of extremist rhetoric and despite the bitterness remaining from Jesse Jackson's 1984 campaign and the overtones of his relationship with Louis Farrakhan, the continuing alliance between agencies and other groups in the Jewish American community and the black-led civil rights groups has remained strong. Whether marching together in fighting racist practices in a county in northern Georgia, issuing joint statements, or proposing common media and legislative strategies, the alliance of the outsider groups in American society, including major Jewish groups, has continued. As the 1984 election results indicated, Jewish voting patterns are more similar to those of black Americans, the main American outsider group, than to those of groups to which Jews are more similar economically. This pattern is not accidental and neither is the statement in 1987 by the leaders of the Conservative Jewish movement in the United States— the most uniquely American of the major American Jewish religious groups—calling for continuing relationships with others interested in civil rights. All of these are patterns of attitudes and behaviors that continue to dominate the actions of the major organizations in American Jewish life.

Also reflecting existing self-perceptions and contributing further to the feelings of being an outsider group are the concern and anxiety among much of the Jewish population in this country regarding the increasingly strong rhetoric and political demands of individuals and groups who appear to be arguing for a "Christianization" of many of our public institutions. Such expressed fears clearly reflect the recognition that their group is essentially outside the mainstream of everyday American existence and that continuing vigilance must therefore be maintained so that our nation's traditional separation of church and state will be maintained. The failure of such vigilance would mean a disappearance of whatever sense of individuality they have as a small, different (Jewish) element within an overwhelming homogeneous (Christian) majority.

A further factor underlying and supporting the feelings of being outsiders is the self-recognition among Jews in this country that they often maintain different religious traditions and institutions, different holidays, and different schools from the majority of American society and that the majority's holidays are more likely to be sanctioned by school and work closings than the holidays celebrated by Jews. There is also the continuing fact of the wearing of skullcaps and the everyday dietary preferences that are practiced by only a minority of Jews but are recognized by all, Jews and non-Jews, as practices that differentiate the two groups.

More important, perhaps, than all of these factors in strengthening Jews' personal and collective feelings of being outsiders and of recognizing that somehow they are different from mainstream America are the historical traditions and the historical memories that Jews transmit through their socializing institutions—traditions that emphasize their status as outsiders in Western culture and the tragic implications of such status over the years. The Inquisition, the Crusades, the Holocaust, and the founding of the State of Israel have all had significance for all of Western culture, for the history of Europe, and for the world in general. However, the history and significance of each of these events are different for Jews than for non-Jews, and it is such differential significance that perhaps most reminds Jews that they are essentially outsiders in major aspects of American life.

The Behavioral Significance of Outsider Status: Equity Motivation and Its Implications

The self-acceptance by Jews of their status as outsiders in American life is one key component underlying their acceptance and sometimes support of equal opportunity and affirmative action programs that may result in discriminatory actions against them. A second key component is the motivational process known as the desire for equitable outcomes. This process can be viewed as the general behavioral tendency to act in a manner that is consistent with self-perceptions and to work to attain outcomes that are consistent or equitable with such self-perceptions.

These action tendencies toward equitable outcomes have long been noted in human behavior and have been used to account for such human behavior as vocational choice processes and work performance, particularly when such actions seem to be contrary to a person's self-interest (Korman, 1970). Though normally not advanced as a framework for understanding motivation in all its varied aspects, the development and continued prominence of equity motivation theory has rested in great part on its ability to help us understand the types of paradoxical, seemingly irrational actions that concern us here (Huseman, Hatfield, and Miles, 1987).

Several major ideas underlie equity motivation theory (sometimes called consistency theory). One assumption is that we first make decisions regarding what outcome would be appropriate for us in a particular situation, and then we engage in actions designed to attain that outcome. A second assumption is that in order to decide what outcome would be appropriate, we compare ourselves either to our previous history or to other individuals and other groups, and on the basis of such comparisons, we make our decision regarding what type of outcome in a particular situation would be equitable or consistent with these self-perceptions. We then engage in the actions designed to attain these outcomes. Among the types of comparisons that are possible, two are of particular relevance here. One comparison is when we match ourselves against an individual (or group) whom we see as similar to ourselves and therefore deserving similar outcomes. If we see ourselves and the similar other individual (or group) actually receiving these similar outcomes, then we are satisfied with the situation. If the outcomes are dissimilar or inequitable, however, tension develops, and we are motivated to change the inputs or outcomes in some way so that we and the "similar other" will have the same outcomes. These changes may include changing our self-perceptions of what we deserve, changing our perceptions of what we believe the others deserve, changing the outcomes either we or the others obtain, or some combination of these, and all of these decisions and consequent behavioral actions take place in the interest of attaining equitable outcomes. A second type of comparison is when we evaluate ourselves against others (individuals or groups) who are different from us along some dimension of importance. In this second case, since the inputs (that is, the characteristics of the others) are different, equity motivation theory suggests that the outcomes must be also different and in the same direction as the differences between the groups. If the outcomes do not follow the same pattern as the inputs, tension arises and actions are taken in order to change either the inputs or the outcomes of the two individuals/groups involved.

If we accept the validity of our assumptions concerning the self-perceptions of Jews as outsiders in American life and the usefulness of equity motivation concepts in understanding choice processes, the paradoxical actions of the Jewish community we have outlined are now more understandable. Underlying such actions may be two types of not necessarily antithetical strategies that have the same impact but rest on different types of comparisons.

Strategy 1: The Desire to Combine with Other Outsider Groups. One strategy rests on the desirability of continually seeking and maintaining alliances with other outsider groups in American society in order to assure the attainment of common long-range goals. The utilization of such a strategy means that, at times, there will be a willingness to accept a "common fate" as appropriate for all outsider groups. This acceptance will include, if necessary, a willingness to "sacrifice"—that is, to accept outcomes and rewards that are appropriate to all outsiders, even if these rewards may be lower than the rewards that might be obtained on an individual basis.

For Jews in the American culture, such alliances need to be made with other outsider groups that are perceived as having a position similar to that of Jews in American society (as outsiders) but whose outcomes (defined as levels of income) are clearly different. In particular, for Jews who believe in adopting this strategy, a problem stems from the fact that Jews are (accurately) perceived by themselves and others as having higher levels of income on the average than their fellow outsiders. The result of such perceptions is the situation pictured in Ratio 1, which describes an inequity that may result in feelings of considerable tension and dissatisfaction that must be reduced by the individuals involved:

Ratio 1

Jewish Americans		*Other Minority Group Americans*
$\dfrac{\text{Outsider Input}}{\text{Outsider Income}}$	$\begin{array}{c}=\\[4pt]>\end{array}$	$\dfrac{\text{Outsider Input}}{\text{Outsider Income}}$

According to the processes underlying equity motivation, inequalities such as those pictured in Ratio 1 will generate motivational pressures to bring the two groups' input/income ratios into line with one another. This goal can be achieved by a number of processes. One way is to attempt to lower the income of the higher group. Another is to increase the income of the individuals or groups at the lower levels by increasing their level of employment.

A third approach is to attempt both processes. Within this context, it can be seen that the support of equal opportunity and affirmative action programs can be viewed as part of a conscious effort to raise the income level of the groups on the right-hand side of the inequality to the level of the group on the left-hand side by increasing the employment levels of the former both quantitatively and qualitatively. However, the evidence we have cited earlier also suggests that another process is possibly being used, perhaps unintentionally, to attain equity between the outsider groups—that is, to bring down the level of income for groups on the left-hand side of the equation. How widespread such an unintended effect may be is open to question, and it is doubtful, of course, that such a negative impact is consciously part of any strategy by a Jewish or non-Jewish group. However, unintended effects of particular strategies are a common implication of organizational decision-making processes, and this is a case in which such unintended effects seem to be occurring.

It may be also noted that this desire to seek equitable outcomes may be strengthened within the Jewish community in this country by the "universalistic" tradition in Judaism, a tradition that encourages those who accept it to work for the rights of others sometimes even more than for themselves. (It must be pointed out that such traditions are not unique to Judaism. They also occur in other cultures and groups. See Weick, Bougon, and Maruyama, 1976; Huseman, Hatfield, and Miles, 1987.) In Judaism, the universalist tradition that Jews have a responsibility to help mankind is exemplified by the statements enunciated by Rabbi Hillel the Elder. The statements are only two brief sentences, but their impact over the years has been enormous. The first sentence is "If I am not for myself, who is for me?" and the second is "If I am only for myself, then what am I?" It is the latter statement that illustrates this particular tradition in Jewish history.

Regardless of where they come from, universalist traditions manifest themselves similarly in reflecting a benevolent, socially concerned way of viewing the world and one's own actions in that world. People who have these views believe that their outcomes relative to input need not be as high as the output/input ratios of others in that they think readily of contributing and giving more and are much less interested in receiving and taking. Regardless of the origins of such attitudes—and they may be cultural, religious, familial, gender-related, or some combination of these (Huseman, Hatfield, and Miles, 1987)—their impact is similar in that they provide important social support for the motivational desire to help increase the outcomes of others. It is a type of support that has historically been part of the Jewish community and that reinforces the processes underlying Ratio 1. It is a way of thinking that is common among many Jews, American and otherwise, and it may have the strategic implications we have suggested.

> Jews, whatever our status, must support the civil, economic and human rights of others for two reasons: It's the right thing to do, and it's good for the Jews. . . .
>
> The existence of a hungry and homeless proletariat is evil in itself; it does not emerge from real democracy, and it will not progress unless democracy makes it possible. It is therefore the role of Jews to strive to feed the hungry. That the job is too big is beside the point. It is also the role of Jews to educate the ignorant, also a big job. It is also our role, and not in our spare time, to make peace. It is not only Jews who have these jobs to do.
>
> The Jews have the unique blessing of helping ourselves when we help others. That probably explains why American Jews are the only group consistently to vote to the left of their wallets (Baritz, 1986, pp. 4).

Strategy 2: The Desire to Avoid Overreward. Less openly acknowledged, perhaps, but also to be expected as a result of the internalization of outsider status by Jews in this country may be a willingness to accept, or at least not protest as vigorously as possible, lower levels of reward than others would demand for the same level of performance (input). Such a lack of protest would block the possible negative consequences that may arise from attaining rewards higher than or equivalent to those of so-called insiders. The processes underlying equity motivation provide the mechanism through which Jews, or other outsiders, may reduce such anxiety. This mechanism can be seen in Ratio 2, which depicts Jews, as outsiders, comparing themselves to non-Jewish insiders in American society according to income levels:

Ratio 2

Jewish Americans		*White Non-Jewish Americans*
Outsider Input	<	Insider Input
Outsider Income	=	Insider Income

In Ratio 2, Jews see themselves as having the same levels of income for a given level of performance as the so-called insiders in American life. Within the structure of equity motivation theory, such perceptions are a source of inequality and are potentially anxiety-producing, since, according to our earlier arguments, insiders are supposed to receive higher levels of return than outsiders.

One way to resolve the resulting tension from the perceived inequality in Ratio 2 is to accept the sacrifice of some income, at least temporarily, until one of two events occurs. One possibility is for the outsider group to change its status and become perceived by themselves and others as insiders. The second possibility is for the outsider group to gain sufficient strength, perhaps in combination with other outsider groups, so that the possible anxieties associated with perceived overreward relative to status can be reduced. Among the mechanisms available for sacrificing income as a result of Ratio 2—a mechanism that would be supported both by the operations of Ratio 1 and by the universalist tradition in Judaism—is the acceptance and/or support of equal opportunity and affirmative action programs.

An Integration

It is important to keep in mind that the explanations we have offered for the paradoxical support of major segments of the Jewish community for equal opportunity and affirmative action programs are only hypotheses at this time. Although they are consistent with what we know and with other known characteristics of Jewish American life—such as the fact that the greatest support for these programs has come from agencies that have been most prominently identified over the years with the civil rights movement and that have continued to work with leaders from other minorities—direct evidence for our proposals is not readily available at this time. We do need such direct evidence, and we should also investigate the possibility that other processes may be involved in the support for these programs in the Jewish community. Whether or not these processes are antithetical to those we have envisaged here, such alternative or additional explanations need further examination.

11
Some Thoughts about Change and Some Continuing Questions

I t seems apparent that the view of Jews as outsiders in the American setting has significantly affected their resulting relationships with corporate America. Most clearly, the American occupational opportunity system has not been working as intended for Jews who are interested in managerial and executive careers. Although Jews have been successful in professional and entrepreneurial roles, and although corporate America has been willing to employ them as professionals, the picture has been far more negative in terms of managerial/executive careers. Also of concern is the apparent willingness to use economic motivation as a basis for the selection or promotion of Jewish job applicants or employees, a pattern that may have put the individuals involved and corporate America at the mercy of those who do not share our values and legal system. When we add these factors to the possibility that the well-publicized success of Jews as professionals and entrepreneurs may be operating as a source of frustration for those who have neither the interest nor capability for these careers and as a source of legitimation of the status quo for those who are not interested in changing corporate America and the declining viability of professional careers in America, we have sufficient reason for a reexamination of much of what has taken place and for a reorientation of the relationship between Jews and corporate America.

There are also other reasons for undertaking such a reassessment. Of particular note is the lack of interest among large segments of the Jewish community in protesting the development and institutionalization of programs on both the societal and corporate levels that have led to a decline in employment opportunities for Jews. It is interesting that this lack of concern seems to exist even though Jews in this country today are probably more strongly identified as Jews and are stronger politically and economically than at any time in their history.

Another factor of major importance that suggests a need for a reexamination is the increasing pressure facing corporate America from third-world competition and technological innovation and the need for change in many traditional ways of thinking and doing business. The importance of corporate America in our economy and in our social structure dictates that it can no longer be allowed, without strong protest, the luxury of attitudes that lead it to use non-effectiveness-oriented criteria for personnel decision making. It hurts the corporations, it hurts the employees, and it hurts the consumer too much—economically, socially, and morally. Finally, and perhaps most important of all, much of what we have said here has to do with the problem of discrimination in corporate America—and any discrimination and lack of equitable opportunity in American life is wrong, regardless of who is doing it and who it is aimed at.

It is desirable on several grounds, then, that this reexamination take place and that changes be encouraged. But what changes? And where do we begin?

What Corporate America Can Do

It would clearly be the height of presumptuous arrogance to suggest that if organizations immediately begin to hire members of the Jewish faith for managerial/executive roles, all, or most, of their problems will be resolved. The argument is ludicrous, unjustified, and unwarranted. Some Jews can make outstanding contributions in managerial/executive roles in resolving the difficulties and meeting the challenges of a particular organization, and some cannot. Attempts to hire and select on the basis of group membership—without due regard for the abilities and competencies of the individuals involved—are wrong morally and are doomed to failure from the viewpoint of effectiveness and competence criteria, regardless of the group involved.

It is not presumptious arrogance, however, to argue that organizations must do away with the kind of thinking that leads them to utilize preexisting group membership categories as a basis for personnel decision making and to avoid selecting or promoting so-called outsiders on that basis alone. This type of thinking is destructive on several counts. Although it is clear that the managerial role calls for interpersonal competence and interpersonal skill, it is arrogant and self-indulgent "insider" thinking to believe that the only individuals who can meet these demands are those who belong to an insider group. This assumption is unwarranted and obviously without justification, regardless of the type of insider-outsider comparison being made. Although it is true in some cases that black Americans will work best with other black Americans and that women will work best with other women, the generalization that this is always true and that it should be used as a basis for personnel decision making is unwarranted and ludicrous.

The use of group membership as a basis for personnel decision making is also demeaning to the nature of the managerial role—a role that demands much more than interpersonal competence. Effectiveness as a manager also requires conceptual vision, entrepreneurial verve, innovativeness, and decision-making capability. It requires an acceptance of responsibility and a competitive urge. The problem is that the selection criterion of social acceptability has too often become the tail that has wagged the dog—a reversal that has operated to the detriment of a society that needs all the managerial skills it can get. It has hurt Jews as well as members of other outsider groups who have not been given a fair shot at managerial/executive career positions in much of corporate America. It has also hurt the corporations that have so emphasized the social acceptability factor that the other necessary managerial characteristics have at times become lost. As a result, our organizations have tended to overemphasize their cultures of agreement and acceptability. They have too often become systems in which the deviant but potentially fruitful thought and the creative idea have difficulty finding a home. In brief, the social acceptability criterion has far too often led organizations to become centers of "groupthink" (Janis, 1972). *Groupthink* is a term that describes the conformity pressures that sometimes so dominate decision making at the executive level that relevant information is screened out, different ideas are censored, and individuals who disagree are forced out of the decision-making process. According to Janis (1972), the results of these processes are often such disastrous decisions as the Bay of Pigs invasion during the Kennedy administration. The social acceptability criterion in executive selection and promotion has far too often led to similar operational processes at the higher levels of many of our major corporations.

One way to bring innovativeness back into organizations is to decrease the importance of the social acceptability criterion as a basis for selecting individuals for managerial/executive career paths in organizations and to include outsiders who may have different ways of thinking but might also meet a social acceptability criterion if given the opportunity. A change of this nature would benefit our organizations and our society as well as our outsider groups, Jews and others. A problem here needs to be recognized however: Corporate America would have to acknowledge, both publicly and to itself, that the criterion of social acceptability as a basis for executive/managerial selection has been important, as has been indicated here, and that other criteria for selection have not been used as often as claimed. Such acknowledgment may not be quick in coming, for it would run counter to the prevailing beliefs of corporate America and those who work with it—such as industrial and organizational psychologists—that rationality and an orientation toward performance effectiveness are dominant ways of thinking in our organizations. Although research study after research study and analysis after analysis have shown that such beliefs are, at best, only partial truths and are often more myth than fact, the claim is still often made that one has been operating rationally even if one has to engage in extensive rationalization processes to defend such claims (DeVries and Miller, 1985; Korman, 1987). In brief, a recognition by corporate America that it has not been operating as rationally as claimed and that the social acceptability criterion has had such overpowering importance in personnel decision making at the managerial/executive level will not be easy to achieve. Difficult as it may be, however, this acknowledgment is necessary if corporate America is to attain the effectiveness of operation that is so crucial for the society in which it exists.

What the American Jewish Community Can Do

The American Jewish community will have to deal with several problems, both individually and through the leadership of the organizations that are so prominently identified with the Jewish population in this country. First, there has been an apparent noninterest in recent years in the lack of managerial/executive opportunities for Jews who wish to develop careers in corporate America. Second, there has been an acceptance, without protest, and often support of the growth of governmental and corporate programs that result in decreasing job and career opportunities for Americans of the Jewish faith.

The lack of interest is surprising in one sense, since, as we have seen earlier, there was great interest in possible patterns of discrimination in corporate employment during the first two decades or so following World War II. More recently, this interest has clearly declined, and there is little research of more contemporary vintage to report. One reason for the decline may be a possible clouding effect of the publicity given to some famous Jewish entrepreneurs and professionals. Although few in number, famous individuals often tend to dominate our consciousness about a particular group, and few of us take the time to look more closely at the realities that underlie what may be misleading surface events. Perhaps, also, there has been a further clouding effect as a result of figures showing that the average level of Jewish income is among the higher groups in the United States. We are a nation in which income level is considered very important, and we often use it as an indication of social and psychological well-being. There are at least two reasons why such thinking may lead to mistaken conclusions. One is that income level is far from being a good indicator of psychological and social well-being. In fact, most of the available evidence suggests that there is a minimal relationship, at best (Korman, in press). A second reason why this type of thinking may lead to mistaken conclusions is that the mean or median score for a group on any variable provides little indication of how low (or high) individual members of that group may score on that variable. The evidence cited in the preceding chapter shows clearly that although Jews as a group have a high income level, large numbers of Jews are below median income levels nationwide and many are below poverty levels. Perhaps another reason for the lack of interest is the belief by some that there is no longer any anti-Semitism in the United States. Such a belief is far from accurate.

Whatever the reason—and there may be other factors involved—there would seem to be a need for a renewal of concern with the lack of Jewish presence in so much of corporate America and the possible contributions of the Jewish community in collaborating unintentionally with the actions that have led to a lack of career opportunities in this area. Discrimination against any group is wrong, and in this case the changing job markets for Jews and other Americans in the professional job markets make it even more important to generate a rebirth of interest in the Jewish presence in corporate America and the conditions that may facilitate or impede such presence.

The second major area of concern for the Jewish community is the need to work toward ending the reverse discrimination against Jews and others that is intrinsic to the types of equal opportunity and affirmative action programs that have been developed during the past two decades and that have now been legalized by Supreme Court decisions (as of this writing). There is a need to end Jews' acquiescence in the development of these programs and a need to end their collaboration with those, Jews or non-Jews, who believe it is acceptable to discriminate against any group.

There is, however, a dilemma that must be dealt with if the elimination of the collaboration with policies leading to reverse discrimination is not to make a bad situation worse. The dilemma stems from the clear fact that invidious discrimination has traditionally been practiced against black Americans, Hispanic Americans, women, and virtually every outsider group in American society. The discrimination has been frequent, widespread, and systemic. It has taken place in all types of personnel decisions, including recruiting, selection, placement, promotion, transfer, demotion, and discharge. There can be no doubt of the facts of such discrimination.

Therefore, what we need to concern ourselves with is the nature of the solution, not the existence of the problem. Can we solve one problem in discrimination by instituting discrimination of another kind? The equal opportunity and affirmative action programs say yes and claim that such discrimination, though perhaps regrettable, is legitimate, is warranted, and must be utilized until, perhaps, sometime in the future when it will no longer be needed (although whether proponents of these programs foresee such an end is not-entirely clear). On the other hand, reason, logic, and a sense of justice tell us that discrimination should never be countenanced, whether it is directed against Jews or anyone else. On an emotional level, discrimination on the basis of group membership—whether it is practiced by an insider group against an outsider or whether it is directed against a member of a group by a Supreme Court ruling—is a violation of our laws, our ethics, and our morality. One wrong does not justify another wrong.

In addition to these considerations, there is another, more pragmatic reason for questioning the value of these programs; that is, an increasing number of empirical research studies have found that these programs do not have the positive effects their proponents claim for them, either for the so-called beneficiaries of the program or for those who are being discriminated against. In fact, the evidence that is beginning to accumulate suggests the contrary:

> When selected on the basis of sex, women devalued their leadership performance, took less credit for successful outcomes, and reported less interest in persisting as a leader; they also characterized themselves as more deficient in general leadership skills. These findings suggest that when individuals have doubts about their competence to perform a job effectively, nonwork-related preferential selection is likely to have adverse consequences on how they view themselves and their performance. (Heilman, Simon, and Repper, 1987, p. 62)

This quotation comes from a study that showed clearly that preferential selection, rather than having positive consequences, had negative effects on the people it was designed to help. It is not the only

research study that has shown such effects. Similar conclusions
have been reached in other experimental studies and in studies in
actual work settings. There is evidence that individuals are judged
more ineffective by others if they are thought to have gained their
jobs through preferential selection (Jacobson and Koch, 1977), and
there is evidence that the job itself becomes less well thought of
when a person obtains it through such means (Heilman and Herlihy, 1984). There is also evidence that women who obtain their
jobs through preferential hiring have higher job stress and lower
job satisfaction (Chacko, 1982).

In brief, a major problem with these programs is that, besides
the moral and ethical dilemmas they pose for those who do not
believe in any sort of discrimination, they simply don't do what
they are supposed to do. Instead of helping the people they are supposed to help, they generate in them such negative feelings as higher
stress and lower self-evaluation, and they encourage other people
to feel more contemptuous of those who are (supposedly) being
helped and the work they are given in a preferential manner. In
addition, they also cause members of other groups to become angry
because they believe that they have lost their jobs unfairly. In the
famous case of a 1985 New York City police sergeants' examination
in which passing grades were altered in order to select more minority group members for the position, a major result was an avalanche
of bitter protests from members of other groups and their families,
who felt they had been deprived unfairly of jobs to which they were
entitled. Thus, the accumulated evidence suggests clearly that these
programs are not worth keeping because they send the wrong sig-
nals both to the people they are supposedly helping and to the
people who are being discriminated against. The signal is that
group membership is what matters, not ability to perform a job.
Group membership as a basis for personnel decision making is un-
worthy of a society that prides itself on achievement, regardless of
whether the group membership criterion is set forth by an insider
group that feels it should control the rewards to be handed out by
that society or by the Supreme Court.

In themselves, these factors would appear to provide sufficient
reasons for Jews *and* non-Jews, working together, to make a con-

certed effort to end these programs in the interest of developing social change programs that will have a better chance of attaining the common goal of a better, more egalitarian society for all. There are also other, more particularistic reasons why Jews, as a group, should work for these goals. Their collaboration with these programs must also be seen as a form of self-abasement. Continued cooperation only further reinforces the view among both Jews and non-Jews that Jews are outsiders in American society who are willing to accept less-than-equitable rewards for their contributions to an organization.

It is also significant that such collaboration may be based, at least in part, on another demonstrably false premise—that anti-Semitism is no longer a major characteristics of American society. According to this justification for such collaboration, Jews, since they no longer need to worry about such difficulties as anti-Semitism in their everyday life, can turn their attention to satisfying the universalist traditions in Jewish life. Like the assumption made by some regarding the beneficial effects of equal opportunity and affirmative action programs on those who are supposedly being helped by such programs, the assumption that anti-Semitism has disappeared from American life is unwarranted.

Contemporary Anti-Semitism in the United States

Clearly, much of a positive nature has taken place in the United States since the end of World War II. Yet such positive signs are not the whole answer, since, in some ways, attitudes and behaviors toward Jews do not seem to have changed very much at all. Anti-Semitic attitudes and behaviors have remained very much part of the American landscape, according to a comprehensive attitudinal assessment of anti-Semitism conducted by a leading American pollster, Daniel Yankelovich, and extensively examined in a monograph by Martire and Clark (1982). Based on 50 in-depth interviews and 1,215 survey interviews in a population of adults aged eighteen and over, the major findings of this study of anti-Semitism in the United States as of about 1980 were as follows:

1. Among non-Jews overall, approximately 23 percent could be classified as prejudiced against Jews, 32 percent were neutral, and 45 percent could be classified as unprejudiced. (Assuming a population of somewhat over 200 million people at the time of the survey, this meant that approximately 50 million people in the United States could be classified as having anti-Semitic attitudes.)

2. Although differences between the sexes and between different religious groups were relatively insignificant, differences between the races were quite large. For whites, 21 percent were classified as prejudiced, 30 percent as neutral, and 49 percent as unprejudiced. For blacks, 37 percent were classified as prejudiced, 41 percent as neutral, and 22 percent as unprejudiced.

3. Anti-Semitism was lower among the young than the old and higher among the uneducated than the educated (except for black Americans, for whom the relationship was reversed). It was also higher in large cities than in smaller cities and towns.

4. In some cases, specific attitudes and beliefs about Jews had become more positive since a previous assessment in 1964; in other instances, they had become more negative. In most cases, however, negative beliefs and attitudes remained high. Table 11–1 summa-

Table 11–1
Non-Jews' Beliefs about Jews in the United States

Belief	Percentage Believing	Percentage Change since 1964
Jews have too much power in U.S.	23	+10
Jews have too much power in business	37	+4
Jews go out of their way to hire other Jews	57	−3
Jews control international banking	43	−12
Jews always like to be at the head of things	52	−11
Jews are willing to use shady practices to get what they want	33	−15
Jews are so shrewd and tricky that others don't have a fair chance in competition	27	−13

Source: G. Martire and R. Clark, *Anti-Semitism in the United States: A Study of Prejudice in the 1980's* (New York: Praeger, 1982), p. 42.

rizes these beliefs and the changes in them since 1964. The first two items show an increased negative view of Jews since 1964; the remaining five show an increased positive view. However, the overall level of negative attitudes remains much higher in the latter group than in the former.

5. In most cases, black Americans viewed Jews considerably more negatively than did white non-Jewish Americans. This reflected a considerable change during the past two decades and suggested a trend leading to possibly even more difficulties between black and Jewish Americans than the problems of the recent past. Table 11–2 shows how strong these changes have been.

6. Twice as many Jews as non-Jews (44 percent versus 22 percent) reported an increased number of anti-Semitic incidents compared to five to ten years previously; a similar number (34 percent and 38 percent) saw about the same number of incidents.

7. Forty percent of the Jewish respondents reported hearing anti-Semitic remarks where they lived or worked; the comparable figure for non-Jews was 13 percent.

Are these figures high or low? There really is no clear answer to this question; it depends on one's expectations. There is less ambiguity, however, if the expectation has been that anti-Semitism is a thing of the past. This is particularly true when we realize that the measures of anti-Semitism used in this study were rather obvious, and answers could be faked by respondents who didn't want

Table 11–2
Beliefs about Jews in the United States: Black/White Comparisons
(percentages)

Belief	1964	1981
Jews stick together too much		
White Non-Jews	53%	51%
Blacks	48%	63%
Jews have too much power in the business world		
White Non-Jews	31%	35%
Blacks	19%	51%

Source: N. Perlmutter and R. S. Perlmutter, *The Real Anti-Semitism in America* (New York: Arbor House, 1982), p. 89.

other people to think that they were anti-Semitic. The conclusions also would have to be negative if we look at the case of black anti-Semitism, a situation that has clearly gotten worse in recent years. Have such attitudes developed among black Americans because the civil rights movement in this country has not been greatly interested in the problem of anti-Semitism and has sanctioned such practices as affirmative action quotas and goals, regardless of their implications for Jewish employment? Or has the civil rights movement merely reflected their constituencies, which have been shaped by other forces into a lack of concern with anti-Semitism, whether generally or in the work setting?

Whatever the reason, this survey clearly shows that anti-Semitic attitudes in this country, even in the few areas where there has been some improvement, remain quite high. Clearly, we are a long way from where we should be, judging from the findings of this study and from other research findings, such as a recent assessment of the attitudes toward Jews of Evangelical Christians (Rothenberg and Newport, 1984), which found that about one-third of this group (about 34 percent) scored from neutral to dislike. Also of relevance to these concerns are the recent comments of Louis Harris, one of America's premier pollsters who has found that as many as 24 percent of Americans living in farm and rural communities exhibit anti-Semitic attitudes and that there is an increasing stridency outside the farm belt when talking about Jews. According to him, Jews who believe that anti-Semitism in this country is a thing of the past are just kidding themselves (Aaron, 1986).

To acquiesce, then, in the development and institutionalization of programs that lead to discriminatory acts against Jews, on the basis of the assumption that anti-Semitism has declined to an insignificant force in American life and that such actions can therefore be tolerated at least temporarily, is an inaccurate reading of the situation and an unjustified assumption. It is not the case when we use attitude measurements.

It is also not the case if we move away from admittedly far-from-perfect attitude measurements and confine ourselves only to relatively objective behavioral indicators. During the mid-1980s there was a host of violent anti-Jewish terrorist groups in the United States—groups that were small in number but were strong enough to murder a Jewish radio talk-show host in Denver and to bomb a Boise, Idaho, synagogue. Although several of these groups were broken up by federal and local police action, there is little reason to think that other groups will not soon rise up to take their place, with the same messages of hate and violence. One area where this had already started to occur by 1985 was among the financially troubled farmers of the American Midwest. During the summer of that year, reports began to be published that a number of violent anti-Semitic groups were beginning to make some headway among farmers by their constant repetition of themes reminiscent of the ideology that influenced much of Henry Ford's anti-Semitism; that is, "It is the Jewish bankers who are responsible for your problems." In fact, the situation became so serious that the ABC-TV program "20/20" devoted a segment of its August 15, 1985, program to these hate groups. The program examined the nature of these groups and showed that violent, almost Nazi-like anti-Semitism remains active and well, even here in the United States. When Geraldo Rivera, the ABC correspondent, showed a picture of Auschwitz victims to one of the farmers, the farmer's first response was to deny the validity of the pictures; then he stated that even if it were true, he "really didn't care very much." Being viewed as a neo-Nazi didn't seem to bother him at all.

Other recent events have, similarly, hardly been encouraging:

1. The growth in the United States (and in Europe) of the so-called revisionist school of historical thought, which denies that the Holocaust ever occurred

2. The distribution at the University of California at Berkeley, one of our most prestigious academic institutions, of the notorious anti-Semitic forgery, *The Protocols of the Elders of Zion*

3. The continued invitations of Louis Farrakhan (a noted anti-Semitic lecturer) to speak at such schools as Wesleyan University and the Universities of Pennsylvania and Maryland, among others

4. The triumph in 1986 Democratic primaries in Illinois of fol-

lowers of Lyndon LaRouche, a notorious anti-Semite who
has preached theories of worldwide economic conspiracies
by a group headed by Queen Elizabeth, the Rockefellers,
and the Jews: Despite such views, two members of his group
were able to win statewide nominations in the Democratic
party in Illinois in that year. One can cite such reasons as a
"surprise" element, overconfidence of other candidates, lack
of knowledge of their real platform, and the like, for their
victory, but the fact remains that they won, and it is not
inconceivable that many of their votes came from people
who knew exactly whom they were voting for.

Anti-Semitism, whether measured attitudinally or behaviorally,
has not disappeared in the United States. It is alive and well, and
those who may have assumed that it does not exist in order to justify support for programs that discriminate against limited numbers
of Jews are acting on incorrect beliefs. Anti-Semitism exists in the
United States of the 1980s, and it must be recognized by individuals
and groups in both the Jewish and the non-Jewish communities.

It is questionable, however, whether such recognition will take
place, for several patterns of American life may operate against the
acceptance of the fact of anti-Semitism in American life. One such
pattern is our apparent need as a culture to believe that income level
equates with well-being. Thus, there are both Jews and non-Jews
who believe that since the financial level of American Jews is above
the norm, their psychological well-being must also be high. The
equality is unwarranted in the general case (Korman, in press), and
there are logical flaws in generalizing group patterns to the individual case. Yet the belief persists. An additional problem that will
hinder the recognition of anti-Semitism in this country by those
who may believe it is minimal is the way in which Jewish life has
been portrayed by the mass media in recent years. In brief, with
rare exceptions (such as the "20/20" program cited earlier), there
has been a continuing lack of media interest in the problems of anti-
Semitism in the United States. For example, no American-made
film has dealt with the problems of anti-Semitism in the United
States in over forty years. In 1947, the film *Gentlemen's Agreement*

was released and the next year the film *Crossfire*. Since then, no American film has dealt with American anti-Semitism.

The problem also involves the manner in which Jews and their life-styles have been portrayed by the mass media. With rare exception, such portrayals have depicted American Jews in stereotypical fashion, with little concern for their problems and the dilemmas they face as outsiders in American life. A common stereotype in television programs, commercials, and the movies is the "JAP" (Jewish American Princess). This characterization is insulting and offensive to the millions of hardworking Jewish women who are career-oriented and family-oriented and who are as concerned as men are with reconciling their needs as individuals, as family members, and as Jews in American society. We also see other negative stereotypes, such as the "Jewish mother" syndrome (for example, in the TV show "Rhoda"), the crass materialistic family with no redeeming values (for example, in the movie *Shampoo*), the affluent Jewish professional (for example, in the TV show "L.A. Law"), and standardized Jewish liberals (for example, in the TV show "Hill Street Blues"). In a wide variety of shows, we see both intermarriage and interrelationships across ethnic lines, without any mention whatsoever of the significance of such relationships for many Jews and the difficulties they may cause both personally and interpersonally. Almost nowhere are there portrayals of stable Jewish family life in America, including religious observances and the problems Jews may face on an everyday basis as citizens of American society. One exception, notable because it stands out so clearly against the general media landscape, is the TV show "St. Elsewhere," which has portrayed a number of sensitive problems in intermarriage and the emotional satisfaction of a dying rabbi's faith. However, such portrayals have been rare, to say the least. In general, the lack of serious, multidimensional examination of the position of Jews in American life—and the resulting lack of knowledge of Jewish life among those who rely on the mass media for much of their information about contemporary America—suggests that acceptance of the reality of anti-Semitism in the American society of the 1980s among both Jews and non-Jews will be more difficult than it would have been had the media spent the past four decades presenting a more accurate, more balanced picture of Jewish life in America.

Resolving the Dilemma

We are faced with a key question. If we grant that the equal opportunity and affirmative action programs to which major segments of the Jewish community have acquiesced and which they have sometimes supported are objectionable on the basis of both lack of demonstrated value and the fact that, intrinsically, they call for reverse discrimination, we are still faced with the problem of responding to the discrimination that generated these programs to begin with. How shall we deal with such discrimination *if* these programs are to be decreased or eliminated?

Key to the establishment of appropriate alternative programs that would have a meaningful chance of success is that they be developed within an appropriate conceptual framework that focuses on and reflects known mechanisms for increasing performance and self-esteem on the part of the individuals involved. Specifically, they should be programs that reflect psychological research on motivation over the years rather than political pressures. One key focus for such a conceptual framework is that the training should be likely to generate an increased sense of self-confidence and self-esteem, an increased willingness to accept responsibility for one's decisions, and an increased desire to achieve.

One reason for the focus on an increased sense of self-esteem and self-confidence is that research has shown consistently that rewards and possibilities of rewards have little impact on the work performance of individuals unless they have the confidence that they can actually attain the rewards being offered. To offer a possibility of increased income to a person who does not believe that he or she has the ability and the competence to attain the reward is not a meaningful way to expect change. The best that can happen under such conditions would be a lack of change. The worst that might happen would be rage and anger on the part of the so-called recipient of the incentive possibilities. To offer an individual something that is not likely to be attainable can only generate increased frustration and increased rage as the person realizes that he or she does not have the ability or competence to attain the reward.

How does one build self-esteem and self-confidence in someone who has little? One way *not* to do it is to increase the person's dependency on others and the person's realization that he or she would not be able to survive save for the largess of others. Such dependency does little except remind the individual of his or her lack of competency, lack of ability to affect his or her own fate, and inability to attain a meaningful career without the help of others. Programs that provide jobs to individuals on the basis of group membership rather than demonstrated or predicted capability fall distinctly into the category of rewards that are undeserved and unwarranted. They offer dispensation of benefits on the basis of largess and the influence of those providing the rewards, and they have little to do with the capability of the individuals receiving the so-called benefits. Furthermore, individuals who are the beneficiary of such rewards are reminded with each benefit given to them of their incapability of taking care of themselves and also of the fact that anything given to them by someone else can also be taken away from them (perhaps just as arbitrarily).

The key idea is to develop different programs—that is, programs that lead individuals to think more of themselves and to value themselves and their competence more highly. Programs that can be designed to achieve these goals are theoretically possible because of our need to utilize both our experiences and the expectations and judgments of others in determining how we feel about ourselves. Such judgments of others may be communicated to us directly or symbolically, but they *are* communicated and they are internalized. The principle is clear, and it has been demonstrated again and again in all types of settings (Korman, 1970): The more others think of people, the more they will think of themselves. The less others think of people, the less they will think of themselves.

One famous illustration of this principle has been called the Pygmalion effect. Eden (1984) reviewed a wide variety of experiments in different settings (though unfortunately few in the work environment) that show clearly that the higher the level of expectations a supervisor or teacher has for individuals, the higher the expectations they have for themselves and the higher their level of performance. In a different but related vein, Korman (1970) has shown the important effect of high self-esteem and self-confidence on work performance and other self-fulfilling choice patterns. Expectancies of others and self-expectancies are related, and they can have a similar impact, because the expectancies of others are social realities that individuals then incorporate into their own sense of self-esteem and self-confidence. The principle is a crucial one; virtually all theories of work motivation stress the importance of self-confidence and high self-expectations in affecting performance levels and the degree to which individuals' choices lead to positive outcomes.

How can we develop programs that attain these goals of a higher sense of self-esteem and, eventually, a greater, more valuable presence of minority groups in the work setting? There is no easy fix. It is a long process. Probably key to the process is increasingly encouraging the individuals involved to be less dependent on the largess of others in resolving life and work problems and to learn how to solve such problems on their own, with less help from others. The training and the development have to start at rather rudimentary levels for those who have little experience in taking care of themselves, but regardless of the level at which it is begun, the process must be instituted and it can be successful. Millions of individuals in this country have learned to take care of their lives and to take control of their fate as a result of life experiences, with or without the help of guided interventions. The development of effective intervention programs can increase the success of such individuals even more. The specifics used in a given situation can vary greatly, according to the people and groups involved, the time available, and other such concrete but important matters. Most important is to keep in mind that the specific program used in helping the development of a sense of self-esteem and self-competence is less important than the necessity of being clear about the goals.

The same idea holds for the development of a willingness to accept responsibility for one's decisions (or the belief in internal control of one's life). The more people believe that they are in control of their lives, the more likely that they will be willing and able to take actions designed to improve their occupational characteristics. The less people believe in such internal control, the less interested they will be in taking appropriate growth-oriented action steps. Clearly, the selection of individuals for jobs and training programs on the basis of group membership rather than individual competence does little or nothing toward building a sense of internal control. In fact, it is most likely that it does the reverse. Here, also, the specifics used in developing such beliefs in internal control are less important than being certain of the goal. It should be noted here that there is some reason to think that the same type of training that is used to build a sense of self-esteem and self-confidence may also have the effect of increasing people's willingness to accept responsibility for their actions. Thus, training programs designed to attain one goal might be expected also to help the attainment of the other (Korman, 1975).

Of these latter training and development programs, programs aimed at increasing achievement motivation in individuals may have the best chance of success at this time. Specific training programs designed to increase internal control and achievement motivation have been developed and have been utilized for at least two decades. Many of these stem from the demonstrated relationship between achievement motivation and successful entrepreneurship (McClelland, 1961). They have been conducted because of the need to develop minority group members and others, including those from other cultures, into more effective entrepreneurs. Although not all of these programs have been successful, a good number have been, and with their clear theoretical rationale and success in some, if not all, instances (McClelland, 1965; McClelland and Winter, 1965), they might be carried further.

One frequently asked question is whether such training programs are possible (or "practical") on a mass basis. There are two answers to this question: (1) we don't know, since few such attempts have ever been made; and (2) the question often reflects the illusion that what we have is working—that is, that equal opportunity and affirmative action programs of the type we have described here have been effective in dealing with the dilemmas of discrimination. The available facts point to just the opposite. The results of these programs have been reverse discrimination and an increased dependency and loss of self-confidence on the part of those who are supposedly being helped. From a practical perspective, then, we have nothing to lose in attempting to implement a different perspective for training and development, since what we have now is perhaps worse than having nothing at all.

Some Continuing Considerations
for the Jewish Community

A most important consideration for the Jewish community is the contemporary implications of being an outsider in American society—both for Jews and for others who can be characterized as outsiders in the same sense. As we have suggested, one of these implications is the impact on career choice processes of seeing oneself and one's group as outsiders. This view seems to increase the value of self-controlled careers, such as the professions or entrepreneurial occupations. Such career opportunities are limited, however, to those who have the abilities, the motivation, and the financial resources to engage in them. Most individuals in the Jewish community, as elsewhere in American society, do not meet these qualifications, and their careers take different paths—shaped by the knowledge that they are members of an outsider group. Our knowledge of the implications of outsider status and how it affects occupational choice and shaping by others is very limited at this time. How does such shaping occur, and where and how do such self-cognitions exert their influence on career (and other kinds of) choices? How do the feelings of being an outsider in corporate America affect the career decision-making patterns of Jewish youth today—both males and, increasingly, females? When do these effects occur, if they do? A number of possibilities suggest themselves. Thus, it may be that childhood socialization patterns in the Jewish community reflect historical and cultural beliefs that tend to encourage children, from their early years, to look only toward professional and entrepreneurial careers and discourage them from managerial/executive careers, even if they are oriented toward such professions. It is extremely significant that if such socialization patterns occur, they may be serving as early sources of discouragement and possible self-stigmatization as failures among those who believe they will never be able to meet the professional or enterpreneurial criterion of success.

It is not inconceivable, however, that some of the discouragement takes place later in life, on college campuses where a Jewish college student who may be oriented toward a management career is told subtly (or perhaps not so subtly) that the oil company interviewing on campus really can't hire any Jewish applicants because of potential problems with the Arab nations (whether this is true or not). These are all questions for which we have few answers at this time except, perhaps, interesting anecdotes and the interpretations of novelists. In the film *The Apprenticeship of Duddy Kravitz,* there is a famous scene in which the loving but bitter Duddy is angry with an older relative whom he believes has mistreated him because he, Duddy, has not been able to attend medical school as his brother has. It is a very emotional, well-played scene, but it is open to question whether it relates to an idiosyncratic event or describes a systematic pattern in childhood socialization patterns among Jewish families in America (and Canada).

It may also be that the problems of being an outsider do not end with the original career decision-making process, important though that process may be. It is not inconceivable that one's entire work life may be affected by such status but that the manner in which such effects would manifest themselves would depend on different job contexts. One interesting question concerns the impact of working in a business organization with a non-Jewish history if one is Jewish and oriented toward a managerial/executive career path. Do such organizations come to be viewed as "enemy camps" with which one must negotiate, often with the aid of allies? As much recent literature has suggested, one does not need to be Jewish in a non-Jewish organization to see the need for allies when one has managerial/executive career aspirations. Is ally-seeking by a Jewish executive in a non-Jewish organization basically the same, or does it differ in some systematic way? The interest in mentors—particularly for women managerial career aspirants—clearly reflects such concerns. The question is whether such processes are affected even further by being Jewish in a non-Jewish organization, perhaps even to the point of seeing such an organization as an enemy camp where one has to tread lightly if one is not to be cast aside. The interviews we reported earlier regarding the need for Jewish executives not to be "too Jewish" suggest that it is not inconceivable that such processes are occurring, but we need more systematic data to detail these processes and the possible social and personal costs of such career patterns more clearly.

Another potential effect suggested by our interviews concerns the possibility of increased personal and social alienation among Jews who commit themselves to managerial/executive careers in non-Jewish organizations. According to this line of thinking, such individuals may become more personally alienated (that is, giving up part of their sense of self) because they agree to be "less Jewish" in the eyes of the organization. They also become socially alienated, because in giving up that part of themselves, they lose contact with the Jewish part of their personal and social history and the social reinforcement such history may provide. In the book *An Orphan in History,* Paul Cowan recounts a touching experience relating to these possible costs, as expressed to him by his father, who, under the name Louis G. Cowan, had risen to the presidency of CBS-TV. After his father had left the TV industry, he began to move back toward his Judaic heritage and talked increasingly to his son of the personal costs of his rise to managerial success. Among these costs were the denial of his Jewish interests and Jewish concerns and, not least, the decision to live under the name Cowan rather than the original family name, Cohen.

The experiences of Louis G. Cowan are the experiences of only one man, however, and although they are suggestive and emotionally provoking, we don't know how widespread such experiences were and how others might have adapted to them differently—if, indeed, other types of response were possible. In effect, we know little of the personal and social costs, if any, of occupational success in contexts where people have denied their heritage. We also know little of the responses of friends and family members to such denials in the social contexts from which they come. We need to know the results (if any) of these compromises as well as the effects on those who remain visibly Jewish in such settings and the responses of their friends and families.

Conclusions

It is necessary to eliminate the belief that because some Jews in the United States have been able to attain a reasonable level of affluence, the problems related to being Jewish in this country have been resolved. The outsider status of Jews in corporate America is as clear now as it has ever been, and noting the average income level of Jews as a group or the publicity surrounding successful Jewish entrepreneurs and professionals does not accurately describe the occupational characteristics of the Jewish community in this country. The outsider status does exist, and it must be recognized as a fact to be dealt with.

One way to deal with such a status is to refuse to accept its negative implications. In recent years there has been a major revival of Jewish identity in this country among people who value their heritage, the particular characteristics of Jewishness, and their contributions to the American society of which they are members. This revival should continue and expand. Individuals who are proud of their identity will not be content with channeling their occupational aspirations only in directions where they need not worry about present and future bosses. Instead, they will move into the careers toward which their interests and abilities guide them, to the benefit of all who are involved. Similarly, they will be less likely to accept a decreased level of the rewards to which they are entitled—a process that distorts the nature of the reward system in general and leads to a distortion of the general operation of the work enterprise. In brief, the development of such a perspective among Jews in American society will increase their value to themselves, to the organizations that employ them, and to the society in which we all live.

References

Aaron, J. (1986). "How Americans View Israel and the Jews." New York: *Jewish Week* 199 (July 18): 4.

Adorno, T. W.; Frenkel-Brunswick, E.; Levinson, D. J.; and Sanford, R. N. (1950). *The Authoritarian Personality*. New York: Harper and Row.

Alba, R. D., and Moore, G. (1982). "Ethnicity in the American Elite." *American Sociological Review* 47: 373–83.

Allport, G. (1954). *The Nature of Prejudice*. Garden City, N.Y.: Doubleday Anchor.

American Jewish Committee. (1967). "Patterns of Exclusion from the Executive Suite: Commercial Banking." New York: American Jewish Committee. Mimeographed, pp. 3–4.

———. (1971). "Discrimination in the Public Utilities Industry—8 Years After." (Draft No. 2). New York: American Jewish Committee, August 12. Mimeographed.

———. (1973). "Summary of Reports on First Fifteen Banks." Report No. 73-610-29. New York: American Jewish Committee. Mimeographed.

American Psychological Association. Awards for Distinguished Scientific Contributions. (1985). *American Psychologist* 40 (March): 285.

Amir, Y. (1969). "Contact Hypothesis in Ethnic Relations." *Psychological Bulletin* 71: 319–42.

Anti-Defamation League. (1963). "Detroit's Old Habit." *ADL Bulletin* 20 (November): 1–2.

———. *ADL Bulletin* 24 (May) 6.

———. (1976). "Jewish Presence in Major U.S. Commercial Banking." Unpublished preliminary report, February.

Asch, S. E. (1956). "Studies of Independence and a Minority of One against a Unanimous Majority." *Psychological Monographs* 70 (9 Whole No. 416).

Baltzell, E. (1964). *The Protestant Establishment*. New York: Vintage Books.

Baritz, L. (1986). "Jews, Labor and Israel." *Na'amat Woman* 1: 4.

Belth, N. C. (1979). *A Promise to Keep*. New York: Times Books.

Belth, N. C. (1981). *A Promise to Keep*. New York: Schocken Books, Inc.

Bennett, R. A. (1986). "Banking Is No Longer Just a WASP Preserve. *New York Times,* June 29, pp. F1, F28.

Birmingham, S. (1984). *The Rest of Us.* New York: Berkely Books.

Blake, R. R., and Mouton, J. S. (1966). "Some Effects of Managerial Grid Seminar Training on Union and Management Attitude toward Supervision." *Journal of Applied Behavioral Science* 2: 387–400.

Blake, R. R.; Mouton, J. S.; and Sloma, R. I. (1965). "The Union-Management Intergroup Laboratory: Strategy for Resolving Intergroup Conflict." *Journal of Applied Behavioral Science* 1: 25–57.

Breer, P., and Locke, E. A. (1965). *Task Experience as a Source of Attitudes.* Homewood, Ill.: Dorsey Press.

Burck, C. G. (1976). "A Group Profile of the Fortune 500 Chief Executives." *Fortune* 93 (May): 173–77.

Business Week. (1986). "The Mysterious 'Coincidences' in Insider Trading Cases." September 8, pp. 76–77.

Chacko, T. (1982). "Women and Equal Employment Opportunity: Some Unintended Effects." *Journal of Applied Psychology* 67: 119–23.

Chronicle of Higher Education. (1986). "Health-Care Shifts Said to Curb Need for New Physicians." 31 (February 4): 1+.

Cohen, S. M. (1983). *American Modernity and Jewish Identity.* New York: Tavistock.

The Corporate 1000. (1985). Washington, D.C.: Washington Monitor.

Cowan, P. (1982). *An Orphan in History.* Garden City, N.Y.: Doubleday.

Cunningham, M. (1983). "Religious Bias Seems Still Strong." *Washington Times,* October 12, p. A5.

Daily News Bulletin. (1986). "Twenty Years Since Nostra Aetate: Study Shows There Is Greater Appreciation of Jews and Judaism in Catholic Educational Institutions." New York: Jewish Telegraph Agency, August 25, p. 4.

Deutsch, M. (1969). "Conflicts: Productive and Destructive." *Journal of Social Issues* 25: 7–41.

De Vries, D. M. F., and Miller, D. (1985). *The Neurotic Organization.* San Francisco: Jossey-Bass.

Domhoff, G. William. (1972). *Fat Cats and Democrats.* Englewood Cliffs, N.J.: Prentice-Hall.

Eden, D. (1984). Self-fulfilling Prophecy as a Management Tool: Harnessing Pygmalion. *Academy of Management Review* 9: 64–73.

Evangelauf, J. (1986a). "Law Deans Blast Hiring Process for Graduates." *Chronicle of Higher Education* 31 (January 5): 1+.

———. (1986b). "Law Schools Boost Recruiting to Offset Application Slump." *Chronicle of Higher Education* 32 (March 5): 1+.

———. (1986c). "Dentistry Schools Striving to Demonstrate That Outlook for Profession Has Improved." *Chronicle of Higher Education* 32 (March 19): p. 3.

Fortune. (1985a. "The Fortune Directory of the 500 Largest Industrial Corporations." 111 (April 29): 252–316.

———. (1985b). "The Fortune Directory of the Largest U.S. Non-Industrial Corporations." 111 (June 10): 266–316.

Freudenheim, M (1986). "A.M.A. Board Studies Ways to Curb Supply of Physicians." *New York Times,* June 14, pp. 1, 15.

Goldberg, A. (1970). "Jews in the Legal Profession: A Case of Adjustment to Discrimination." *Jewish Social Studies* 32 (April): 148–61.

Greenhaus, J. H.; Korman, A. K.; and Gavin, J. F. (1974). "Perceptions of Organization Climate, Tenure and Job Attitudes." Unpublished manuscript, Baruch College, CUNY.

Grossman, E. (1986). "The Search for the Third Way." *Jerusalem Post International Edition,* September 27, pp. 17–18.

Grossman, L., and Stenig, M. (1985). "Jewish Involvement in Top Corporate Management in Philadelphia, 1984." Unpublished manuscript. Philadelphia: American Jewish Committee, March 31.

Guetzkow, H. (1965). "The Creative Person in Organizations." In G. Steiner (ed.), *The Creative Organization.* Chicago: University of Chicago Press.

Harr, J. (1985). "Secrets: The Hidden World of Harry Gray." *New England Monthly,* October, pp. 37–44, 91, 93–97.

Hartely, J. (1984). "Industrial Relations Psychology." In M. Gruneberg and T. Wall (eds.), *Social Psychology and Organizational Behavior.* Chichester, England: Wiley, pp. 149–82.

Heilman, M., and Herlihy, J. H. (1984). "Affirmative Action, Negative Reaction? Some Moderating Conditions." *Organizational Behavior and Human Performance* 33: 204–13.

Heilman, M.; Simon, M. C.; and Repper, D. P. (1987). "Intentionally Favored, Unintentionally Harmed? Impact of Sex-based Preferential Selection on Self-Perceptions and Self-Evaluation." *Journal of Applied Psychology* 72: 62–68.

Hilberg, R. (1961). *The Destruction of the European Jews.* Chicago: Quadrangle.

Huseman, R. C.; Hatfield, J. D.; and Miles, E. W. (1987). "A New Perspective on Equity Theory: The Equity Sensitivity Construct." *Academy of Management Review* 12: 222–34.

Isaacs, S. (1974). *Jews and American Politics.* Garden City, N.Y.: Doubleday.

Jacobson, M. B., and Koch, W. (1977). "Women as Leaders: Performance Evaluation as a Function of Leader Selection." *Organizational Behavior and Human Performance* 20: 149–57.

Janis, I (1972). *Victims of Groupthink.* Boston: Houghton-Mifflin.

Jenkins, D. (1973). *Job Power.* Garden City, N.Y.: Doubleday.

Jewish Currents. (1986). "Inside the Jewish Community: Jews and Affirmative Action." 40 (May): 30–31.

Jewish Life on Campus. (1985). Washington, D.C.: B'nai B'rith Hillel Foundation.

Johnson, D. (1986). "Yale's Limit on Jewish Enrollment Lasted Until early 1060's, Book Says." *New York Times,* March 4, pp. B1, B5.

Kerr, C., and Siegel, A. (1954). "The Inter-Industry Propensity to Strike: An International Comparison." In A. Kornahauser, R. Dubin, and A. Ross (eds.), *Industrial Conflict.* New York: McGraw-Hill.

Kipnis, D. (1976). *The Power Act.* Chicago: University of Chicago Press.

Korman, A. (1963). "Selective Perception Among First-Line Supervisors." *Personnel Administration* 26: 31–36.

———. (1970). "Toward a Hypothesis of Work Behavior." *Journal of Applied Psychology* 54: 31–41.

———. (1971a). "Environmental Ambiguity and Locus of Controls as Interactive Influences on Satisfaction." *Journal of Applied Psychology* 55: 339–42.

———. (1971b). "Organizational Achievement, Aggression and Creativity: Some Suggestions Toward an Integrated Theory." *Organizational Behavior and Human Performance* 6: 593–613.

———. (1975). "Work Experience, Socialization and Civil Liberties." *Journal of Social Issues* 31: 137–51.

———. (1987). "Irrational Behavior and Its Implications for Organizational Behavior Theory." Paper presented at Second Annual Meeting of the Society for Industrial and Organizational Psychology, Atlanta, Georgia.

———. (In press). "Theories of Career Success and Personal Failure." *Journal of Occupational Behavior.*

Kornhauser, A. (1965). *Mental Health of the Automobile Worker.* New York: Wiley.

Krefetz, G. (1982). *Jews and Money.* New Haven and New York: Ticknor and Fields.

Landau, D. (1984). *The Jewish Book of Lists.* Briarcliff Manor, N.Y.: Stein and Day.

Levison, A. (1974). *The Working-Class Majority.* New York: Coward, McCann and Geoghegan.

Lipman, S. (1984). "Spunky Jewish Educator Wins Round in Discrimination Battle." *Jewish Week* 194 (December 21): 14.

Lipstadt, D. E. (1985). *Beyond Belief: The American Press and the Coming of the Holocaust, 1933–1945.* New York: Free Press.

Lundberg, F. (1968). *The Rich and the Super-Rich.* New York: Bantam.

Maier, N. R. F., and Hoffman, R. (1961). "Organization and Creative Problem-solving." *Journal of Applied Psychology* 45: 277–80.

Martire, G., and Clark, R. (1982). *Anti-Semitism in the United States: A Study of Prejudice in the 1980's.* New York: Praeger.

McClelland, D. (1961). *The Achieving Society.* Princeton, N.J.: Van Nostrand.

———. (1965). "Toward a Theory of Motive Acquisition." *American Psychologist* 20: 321–33.

McClelland, D., and Winter, D. (1965). *Motivating Economic Achievement.* New York: Free Press.

McComas, M. (1986). "Atop the Fortune 500: A Survey of the C.E.O.'s." *Fortune* 113 (April 28): 26–31.

Michael, R. (1985). "America and the Holocaust." *Midstream* 31 (February): 13–16.

Milgram, S. (1974). *Obedience to Authority.* New York: Harper and Row.

Miller, J. (1986). "Erasing the Past: Amnesia About the Holocaust." *New York Times Magazine,* November 16, pp. 31–36, 40, 109–111.

Miller, W. (1952). "American Historians and the Business Elite." In William Miller (ed.), *Men in Business.* New York: Harper and Row, pp. 311–24.

Mills, C. Wright. (1959). *The Power Elite.* New York: Oxford University Press.

Morse, S. (1987). "The Christianization of America: How Serious a Threat?" *Jewish Monthly* 101 (5): 18–22, 27–28.

Newcomer, M. (1955). *The Big Business Executive.* New York: Columbia University Press.

———. (1986). "Engineer Wins Job Discrimination Suit." 198 (April 25): 7.

———. (1987). "Jewish Jobless." 199 (January 16): 4.

New York Times. (1963). December 29, p. 1+.

Perlmutter, N., and Perlmutter, R. S. (1982). *The Real Anti-Semitism in America.* New York: Arbor House.

Powell, R. M. (1969). *Race, Religion, and the Promotion of the American Executive.* Columbus: Ohio State University Press.

Prager, D., and Telushkin, J. (1983). *Why the Jews?* New York: Simon and Schuster.

Quinley, H. E., and Glock, C. Y. (1979). *Anti-Semitism in America.* New York: Free Press.

Quinn, R. P.; Kahn, R. K.; Tabor, J. M.; and Gordon, L. K. (1968). *The Chosen Few: A Study of Discrimination in Executive Selection.* Ann Arbor: University of Michigan, Institute for Social Research.

Rights. (1959). "Employment in Insurance Companies." 2 (November-December): 59–62. New York: Anti-Defamation League.

———. (1963). "Employment of Jewish Personnel in the Automobile Industry." 5 (October). New York: Anti-Defamation League.

———. (1967). "Discrimination in Employment." 6 (June): 117–18. New York: Anti-Defamation League.

———. (1968). "Employment Discrimination in Big Business." 7 (February): 121–26. New York: Anti-Defamation League.

———. (1978). "A Study of Jewish Employment Problems in the Big Six Oil Company Headquarters." (Summer). New York: Anti-Defamation League.

Ritterband, Paul, and Cohen, Steven M. (1983). "The Social Characteristics of the New York Area Jewish Community, 1981." In M. Himmelfarb and D. Singer (eds.), *American Jewish Yearbook, 1984.* New York: American Jewish Committee.

———. (1984). "Sample Design and Population Estimation: The Experience of the New York Jewish Population Study, 1981–1984." In S. M. Cohen, J. S. Woocher, and B. A. Phillips (eds.), *Perspectives in Jewish Population Research.* Boulder, Colo., and London: Westview Press.

Rosenblatt, G. (1985). "Good News, Bad News for American Jews." *Baltimore Jewish Times,* May 24, pp. 40–43.

Rothenberg, S., and Newport, F. (1984). *The Evangelical Voter: Religion and Politics in America*. Washington, D.C.: Free Congress Research and Education Foundation.

Rottenberg, D. (1979). "How to Succeed in Business Without Being Gentile." *Jewish Living,* December, pp. 39–43.

Rubin, I. (1967). "Increased Self-Acceptance: A Means of Reducing Prejudice. *Journal of Personality and Social Psychology* 5: 223–38.

Sellers, P. (1985). "America's Most Admired Corporations." *Fortune,* 111, January 7, 1: pp. 18–33.

Silberman, C. E. (1985). *A Certain People: American Jews and Their Lives Today.* New York: Summit Books.

Slavin, S. L., and Pradt, M. S. (1982). *The Einstein Syndrome: Corporate Anti-Semitism in America Today*. Lanham, Md.: University Press of America.

Smircich, L. (1983). "Concepts of Culture and Organizational Analysis." *Administrative Science Quarterly* 28: 339–58.

Spiegel, J. (1963). "Anti-Jewish Bias Laid to Utilities." *New York Times*. Dec. 29: pp. 1, 27.

Stapp, J.; Tucker, A. M.; and VandenBos, G. R. (1985). "Census of Psychological Personnel: 1983." *American Psychologist* 40(12): 1317–51.

Stephan, W. G., and Brigham, J. (1985). Intergroup Contact: Introduction. *Journal of Social Issues* 41(3): 1–8.

Sturdivant, E., and Adler, R. (1976). "Executive Origins: Still a Grey Flannel World?" *Harvard Business Review,* November-December, pp. 125–33.

Taylor, S., Jr. (1986). "Affirmative Action Upheld by High Court as a Remedy for Past Job Discrimination." *New York Times,* July 2, pp. A1, B9.

———. (1987). "Supreme Court, 6-3, Extends Preferences in Employment for Women and Minorities. *New York Times,* March 26, p. A1 +.

Tomchin, S. (1985). "BBW Board Votes to Support Affirmative Action Goals." *Womens World* 76 (October-November):1, 4.

Volkman, E. (1982). *A Legacy of Hate: Anti-Semitism in America*. New York: Franklin Watts.

Waldman, L. (1956). "Employment Discrimination against Jews in the United States. . . . 1955." *Jewish Social Studies* 18: 3.

Waxman, C. (1983). *America's Jews in Transition*. Philadelphia: Temple University Press.

Weick, K.; Bougon, M; and Maruyama, G. (1976). "The Equity Context." *Organizational Behavior and Human Performance*. 15: 32–65.

Welles, C.; Templeman, J.; and Cohan, V. (1986). "The Mysterious 'Coincidences' in Insider Trading Cases." *Business Week*. September 8: pp. 76–77.

Wyman, D. S. (1984). *The Abandonment of the Jews*. New York: Pantheon Press.

Zweigenhaft, R. L. (1980). "American Jews: In or Out of the Upper Class?" In G. W. Domhoff (ed.), *Power Structure Research*. Beverly Hills, Calif.: Sage, pp. 47–70.

———. (1982). "Recent Patterns of Jewish Representation in the Corporate and Social Elites." *Contemporary Jewry* 6(1): 36–46.

———. (1984). *Who Gets to the Top? Executive Suite Discrimination in the Eighties.* New York: American Jewish Committee Institute of Human Relations.

Zweigenhaft, R. L., and Domhoff, G. W. (1982). *Jews in the Protestant Establishment.* New York: Praeger.

Copyright Acknowledgments

Subject Index

Affirmative action: employment programs, 119, 141–142, 160; impact of, 171–173, on Jewish women, 145, on Jewish employment, 149–152

Antisemitism: American patterns, historical, 7–11, recent, 11–15; behavioral manifestations, 176–178; among black Americans, 174–175; European patterns, recent,7; political and ideological patterns, 6

Arab boycott: and Jewish employment, 126–130; legal remedies of, 128–129

Automobile industry and Jewish employment patterns, 54

Authoritarian personality, 139

Banks and corporate recruiting, 104

Chief executive officers, Jewish, 58–60, 84–87

Christianization of American movements, 12, 156

College discrimination against Jews, 108–111

Commercial banking and Jewish employment, 44–45, 49–51, 79–82

"Contact" Hypothesis, 13

Corporation acceptance of Jewish professionals, 114–116

Corporate recruiting patterns and Jewish employment, 92–96, 99–102

Economic motivation: impact on discrimination, 125–126, 129–130

Employment: expected levels of Jewish, 88–89; patterns of I–0 psychologists, 116–118

Entertainment industry: and Jewish employment, 22–23; and Jewish identification, 21–23

Entrepreneurial spirit and Jewish socialization practices, 17–20

Equal-opportunity programs, 141–142, 160

Equity motivation, 157–162

Executive recruiters and antisemitism, 98

Fashion industry, Jewish contributions to, 21–23

F-scale, 139–140

Fortune 500: comparisons in proportions of Jewish executives, company, 74–76, industry, 70–74; recruiting practices, 104

Fortune 100: comparisons in proportions of Jewish executives, company, 74–76

Fortune Service 500: comparisons in proportions of Jewish executives, industry, 78–80

Group categorization and employment decisions, 142–147

"Groupthink," 168

Hierarchical organizations and attitudes toward outsiders, 133–134

Industry structural characteristics and proportions of Jewish executives, 76
Insurance industry: and Jewish employment patterns, 44–45, 51–53, 79; recruiting practices, 104
Intellectual careers among Jews, 113–114
Internal-control training programs, 182–183

Jewish acceptability: as managers, 29–32; in organizations, 33–34, 38–39
Jewish contributions to retailing industry, 21–23
Jewish employment: how Jewish "history" has an impact on, 85–87
Jewish family influences, 65
Jewish representation on corporate boards, 57, 59–60
Jewish responses: to affirmative-action programs, 152–154, 165–166; to antisemitism, 6
Jewish self-perceptions as outsiders, 154–157
Jewish traditions: and entrepreneurialism, 19–20; and "portable" careers, 21

Labor market patterns of the professions, changes in, 120–123
Leadership influence on hostility to others, 134–135

Managerial role and demand for social acceptability, 167–169
Media descriptions of Jews in American life, 14

"Names" method in estimating Jewish proportions of sample groups, 66–70
"Nativist" tradition in American literature, 14

Organizational characteristics and attitude toward outsiders, 133–134

Outsider status: and behavioral implications, 1–3, 157–163; of Jewish executives, 184–187; and the managerial role, 27–29
Overt discrimination against Jews: in employment contexts, 32–33, 36–38, 44–45, 47–49

Petroleum industry: and affirmative action, 147–149; and Jewish employment, 126–127
Professional occupations and social acceptability, 107–108
Professional success and its effects, 112–114

Quota systems in colleges and professional schools, 108–111

Retailing industry and Jewish employment, 79, 83
Reverse-discrimination, 141–144

Selection ratios in corporate recruiting decisions, 97
Self-esteem: and performance, 180–181; and training programs, 181–184
Service industries: company comparisons in Jewish employment patterns, 79, 83
Shipping industry and Jewish employment, 53–54
Social acceptability and the managerial role, 28–29
Supermarket industry and Jewish employment, 79, 83–84
Supreme Court decisions on affirmative-action, 141–144

"Universalist" tradition in Judaism, 160–161
Urban-rural campus locations and corporate recruiting, 95–96
Utilities industry and Jewish employment, 44–45, 54–55, 79
Utilities industry, recruiting practices, 104

Views of Jews as different, 13–14

Name Index

Aaron, J., 176
Abrams, L. M., 128
Abzug, B., 214
Adler, R., 62, 69
Adorno, T. W., 139
Alba, R. D., 62, 69
Amir, Y., 139
Arrow, K., 119
Asch, S. E., 155

Baritz, L., 161
Bellow, S., 114
Belth, N. C., 45, 54, 111, 121, 144
Bennett, R. A., 62, 69, 131
Bickel, A., 144
Bienstock, H., 151
Birmingham, S., 130
Blake, R. R., 138
Blaustein, E. 24
Bougon, M., 160
Breer, P., 136
Brigham, J., 139
Brody, S., 57
Bronfman, E., 24
Brown, J. F., 10
Brown, M., 113
Burck, C. G., 58, 59

Cahan, V., 13
Chacko, R., 172
Clark, R., 173, 174
Cohen, S. M., 69, 80, 151
Conant, J. B., 109
Cowan, P., 186
Crown, H., 24

Cummings, N., 25
Cunningham, M., 88

Deutsch, M., 138
De Vries, D. M. F., 168
Domhoff, G., 57, 59, 69, 84, 87, 88

Eden, D., 181
Englehard, C., 24
Evangelauf, J., 121

Farrakanh, L., 155, 177
Firestone, S., 144
Ford, H., 45, 46, 88, 177
Freidan, B., 114
Friedman, M., 114
Frenkel-Brunswick, E., 139
Freudenheim, M., 121
Fribourg, M., 24

Gavin, J. F., 137
Goldberg, A., 112
Goldstein, J., 113
Goldwyn, S., 23
Gordon, L. K., 32, 33, 135
Gray, H. J., 67, 68
Greenhaus, J. H., 137
Griswold, D., 110
Grossman, E., 14
Grossman, L., 63
Gudeman, E., 86
Guetzkow, H., 138

Hammer, A., 24
Harr, J., 68
Harris, L., 176

Hart, W. S., 111
Harteley, J., 2
Hatfield, J. D., 157, 160, 161
Heilman, M., 171, 172
Herlihy, J. H., 172
Hess Family, 24
Hilberg, R., 5
Hochberg, M., 129
Hoffman, R., 138
Huuseman, R., 157, 160, 161

Jacobson, M., 172
Jackson, J., 155
Janis, I., 168
Jenkins, D., 110

Kahn, R. L., 32, 33, 135
Kerr, C., 114
Kipnis, D., 133,134
Klein, L., 114
Koch, W., 172
Korman, A., 137, 138, 139, 157,
   168, 169, 178, 183
Kornhauser, A., 137
Krefetz, G., 17, 18, 113
Krulik, D., 149, 150

Ladd, W. S., 111
Landau, D., 112
LaRouche, L., 178
Lautenberg, F., 25
Lear, N., 23
Lefrak, S., 24
Levinson, D. J., 139
Levison, A., 137
Linde, S. A., 128
Lipstadt, D. E., 9
Locke, E. A., 136
Lowell, A. L., 108
Lundberg, F., 88

Maier, N. R. F., 138
Martire, G., 173, 174
Maruyama, G., 160
Mayer, L. B., 23
McClelland, D., 19, 183
McComas, M., 59
Miles, E. W., 157, 160, 161

Milgram, S., 134
Miller, D., 168
Miller, J., 7
Miller, W., 58
Mills, C. W., 88
Moore, G., 62, 69
Morse, S., 12
Mouton, J. S., 138
Muensterberg, H., 116

Newport, F., 176
Newcomer, M., 58

Ochs, A., 87
Oren, D., 109

Paley, W., 23
Pavlevsky, M., 25
Perlmutter, N., 174
Perlmutter, R., 174
Powell, R. H., 30, 31, 32, 33
Pradt, M. S., 66, 82, 92, 94, 95, 96,
   97, 98, 99, 104, 106, 115, 148
Prager, D., 113
Pritzker, J., 57
Pritzker Family, 24

Quinn, R. P., 32, 33, 135

Ramos, S., 25
Repper, D. P., 171
Revson, C., 24
Rifkind, S., 57, 85
Ritterband, P., 69, 151
Rosenblatt, G., 150
Rosenwald, L., 130
Rothenberg, S., 176
Rottenberg, D., 63, 86, 115
Rubin, I., 138

Samuelson, P., 113
Sanford, R. N., 139
Sarnoff, D., 23
Scalia, A., 144
Schapiro, J., 24
Scheinfeld Family 24
Schneider, S. W., 114
Sellers, P., 70
Shapiro, I., 85

Shorenstein, W., 24
Siegel, A., 138
Silberman, C., 10, 19, 111, 113
Simon, M., 24
Simon, M. C., 171
Singer, I., 114
Slavin, S., 66, 82, 92, 94, 95, 96, 97, 98, 99, 104, 106, 115, 148
Sloma, R. L., 138
Smirchich, L., 133
Smith, C. J., 24
Spiegel, J., 55
Stapp, J., 121
Stenig, M., 63
Stepan, W. G., 139
Stern, L., 24
Stollman, M., 24
Stollman, P., 24
Sturdivant, E., 62, 69
Sulzberger, A., 87
Swig, B., 25

Tabor, J. M., 32, 33
Tajfel, H., 2
Taub, M., 25
Taylor, S., Jr., 144, 148
Telushkin, J., 113
Templeman, J., 13

Tisch, L., 17, 18
Tomchin, S., 153
Tucker, A. H., 121

Vandenbos, G. R., 121
Vidal, G., 14
Volkman, E., 128
Vorspan, A., 152, 153

Waksman, S., 128
Waldman, L., 48
Warner Bros., 23
Waxman, C., 150
Weick, K., 160
Weinberg, S., 85
Welles, C., 13
Werner, J., 24
Wexner, L., 17, 18
Winter, D., 183
Winters Family, 24
Wood, R., 86
Wyman, D., 9

Yalow, R., 113
Yankelovich, D. G., 173

Zweigenhaft, R. L., 34, 35, 57, 59, 60, 69, 84, 85, 87

About the Author

D r. Abraham K. Korman is the Wollman Distinguished Professor of Management at Baruch College, City University of New York. He is the author of *Career Success and Personal Failure, Psychology of Motivation, Management Development in a Changing World,* and approximately fifty articles in the areas of work motivation, leadership decision making, and management and organizational development. Dr. Korman has consulted to such Fortune 500 companies as Beatrice Foods, the Fairchild Corporation, IBM, American Airlines, Amstar, Lever Brothers, RCA, and Tribune Publishing and has lectured in Great Britain, the Netherlands, Egypt, Israel, and China.